T0368103

CHERRY BLOSSOMS
AND
TIDAL WAVES

KEN BOARD

WESTBOW
PRESS®
A DIVISION OF THOMAS NELSON
& ZONDERVAN

WestBow Press books may be ordered through booksellers or by contacting:

WestBow Press
A Division of Thomas Nelson & Zondervan
1663 Liberty Drive
Bloomington, IN 47403
www.westbowpress.com
844-714-3454

Scripture quotations are taken from the King James Version, public domain.

ISBN: 979-8-3850-3945-6 (sc)
ISBN: 979-8-3850-3944-9 (e)

Library of Congress Control Number: 2024925480

Print information available on the last page.

WestBow Press rev. date: 12/19/2024

CONTENTS

A DIFFERENCE OF 189 POUNDS

I sat down and turned on the TV to watch sumo. When the two sumo wrestlers stepped into the ring, I laughed. One of them weighed 218 pounds. The other one weighed 407 pounds. A difference of 189 pounds! I thought, "This match will be over quickly."

At first, the larger wrestler grabbed hold of the smaller wrestler, but the smaller man used his speed to get behind his opponent and push him out of the ring. I shouted with excitement along with everyone else.

When I saw this match, which Bible story do you think I remembered? Right, the story of David and Goliath written in chapter seventeen of First Samuel.

According to verse 4, Goliath was over nine feet tall. David was just a youth. Goliath was a soldier. David was a shepherd. Their battle should have ended quickly in an overwhelming victory for Goliath. However, as you know, David was able to defeat Goliath.

David explained the key to his victory in verse 45. "Thou comest to me with a sword, and with a spear, and with a shield: but I come to thee in the name of the Lord of hosts, the God of the armies of Israel, whom thou hast defied." Because David was assured of God's presence with him, he was able to fight valiantly and gain the victory;

Because the Christian knows that God is with him, no matter how ferocious a "giant" he meets in his daily life, he can gain the victory through the power that God gives him. "If God be for us, who can be against us?" (Romans 8:31)

A MEAL IN HEAVEN

Last Sunday afternoon I enjoyed a delicious meal at the home of Brother and Sister Koh. For several hours we ate and talked and laughed. Sister Koh prepared a splendid meal. There were three kinds of curry – Japanese, Malaysian and Indian. It was the first time for me to eat Malaysian curry and Indian curry. They were very delicious.

There was also an Indian bread called *nan* and some salad. When I was already quite full, they brought out some watermelon and cream puffs. Just when I thought I could not eat any more, another couple arrived with sandwiches and pudding. My stomach enjoyed the delicious food and my soul was encouraged by the fellowship.

During the meal someone asked, "Will we eat in heaven?" According to Revelation 19:6-7, the next event after the rapture will be the marriage supper of the Lamb. "And I heard as it were the voice of a great multitude, and as the voice of many waters, and as the voice of mighty thunderings, saying, Alleluia: for the Lord God omnipotent reigneth. Let us be glad and rejoice, and give honour to him: for the marriage of the Lamb is come."

Recently I was asked, "What is the best meal you have ever had?" I didn't have to think long. It was a meal at a Mexican restaurant called Rosita's in Fukuoka City in Japan. My mouth still waters for the enchiladas and tacos that they serve there.

Some day we shall have a meal a hundred times more delicious than anything we have eaten before. Imagine the meal that God shall prepare at the marriage supper of the Lamb for all people who believe in Christ.

A REAL HERO

The heroes of this world are people like athletes, singers, and movie stars, Last Sunday I met a real hero.

She does not play any sport. She does not have a beautiful voice that entertains people. She has never appeared in a movie. The truth is, she is already 77 years old. Her hair is gray. Her back is slightly bent. When she walks, she has to use a cane.

"She" is Missionary Hiroko Matsumoto who has been serving the Lord in West Africa for the past 28 years. When they reach the age of 50, many people begin to think of retirement. At the age of 50, Miss Matsumoto surrendered her life to the Lord and went to Senegal.

I asked her, "Are you about ready to retire?" She replied, "I am going back to Senegal in May." When I heard her reply, I remembered the words written in Acts 15:25-26. "Barnabas and Paul, men that have hazarded their lives for the name of our Lord Jesus Christ." We could put the name of Hiroko Matsumoto in the place of the names of Barnabas and Paul.

At church we often use the word "surrender." As I watched Miss Matsumoto leave the church, I thought, "That is the image of surrender." In spite of age or the circumstances of life, the person who obeys the leadership of the Lord and does His will is the person who has truly surrendered his life to the Lord.

"Present your bodies a living sacrifice, holy, acceptable to God, which is your reasonable service." (Romans 12:1)

A SPECIAL VIOLA

On July 7th Gakushin University graduate students' orchestra performed a concert. One of the graduates who participated in the concert played a very special viola made from a "miracle tree" that withstood the tidal waves. There is a picture of that tree on the back of the viola.

Muneyuki Nakazawa made this violin. He also made a violin out of the rubble. He plans to have one thousand musicians play this instrument.

When I heard this story, I remembered the words of a song:

"Something beautiful, something good
All my confusion, Jesus understood
All I have to offer Him is brokenness and strife
But He made something beautiful out of my life."

The Bible passage that gave birth to this song is Isaiah 61:3. "To appoint unto them that mourn in Zion, to give unto them beauty for ashes, the oil of joy for mourning, the garment of praise for the spirit of heaviness." In the Old Testament period, people who were saddened often put ashes on their head. (Ezekiel 4:3; Job 2:8) When Isaiah wrote this passage, he referred to this custom.

God is able to take a life that resembles a pile of rubble left by a tidal wave and make something beautiful out of it. David wrote about this experience in Psalm 30:11. "Thou hast turned for me my mourning into dancing: thou hast put off my sackcloth, and girded me with gladness."

When the experiences of life have left you in ruins, bring your life to God and let Him make something beautiful out of it.

KEN BOARD

A STRANGE ATMOSPHERE

To prevent the increase of Covid patients, right now many sports events are being held without fans. The spring sumo tournament is one of those events. Have you ever watched sumo when there were no fans? When I watched the first day of the tournament on TV, I was amazed. It was truly a strange atmosphere. It was so quiet the shouts of the referee echoed throughout the arena.

The fans were not the only ones who sensed the strange atmosphere. Even the wrestlers were affected by the silence. One of them said, "The will to fight just wasn't there, I thought, 'What am I fighting for?'"

When I read his words, they caused me to think about the importance of Christians encouraging one another. Although I am a missionary, there are times when I lose the will to fight. Do you have times like that? When we face a painful trial, or when the results of our evangelism are not the results we desired, we many lose the will to fight for the Lord and for the gospel.

In times like these, it is the voice of encouragement of other Christians that restores our will to fight. "Do not be discouraged. Hang in there! The Lord is with you. If God be for us, who can be against us?" (Romans 8:31)

This may be a strange way of saying it, but the church should be the fan club of the Christian. Let's receive strength by cheering each other on and fight the good fight of faith. "Not forsaking the assembling of ourselves together, as the manner of some is; but exhorting one another: and so much the more, as ye see the day approaching." (Hebrews 10:25)

A TERRIFYING THREE HOURS
AT THE POLICE STATION

———— ❧ ————

Many years ago, when a foreigner renewed his alien registration certificate, he was required to go to the ward office within two weeks and report the renewal. One time, I went to the ward office a month after I renewed my certificate. The ward office official said, "You are two weeks late, so the police may come to your home." I thought, "The police will not come to my home just because I was two weeks late in reporting the renewal of my certificate."

A few days later, a detective came to my home and said, "You have violated the Alien Registration Certificate Law. You must come to the police station." When we arrived at the police station, two detectives were waiting for us. One of them took my wife to a separate room to interrogate her. The detective began with the question, "Where were you born?" and for the next three hours he asked me many questions. Finally, I was able to convince him that I had just forgotten to report the renewal within the two-week time limit. The investigation ended with just a warning, but it was such a terrifying experience that ever since then I always report the renewal within two weeks.

According to the Bible, all Christians will undergo a similar investigation. Of course, the soul of the Christian is eternally secure, but in Second Corinthians 5:10 it is written, "For we must all appear before the judgment seat of Christ; that every one may receive the things done in his body, according to that he hath done, whether it be good or bad." Therefore, let us live a life that is pleasing to the Lord so that we will not have to be afraid when we stand before His judgment seat. "Abide in him; that, when he shall appear, we may have confidence, and not be ashamed before him at his coming." (First John 2:28)

KEN BOARD

A TRAIL OF SOY SAUCE

A friend staying at my home for a while bought some soy sauce. When he returned home, he left the soy sauce in my refrigerator, but I rarely use soy sauce, so I put the bottle into a bag and took it to church.

I did not notice it, but the bottle was not closely tightly, so some of it spilled into the bag. I thought it would be better to wash the bottle off before I put it into the refrigerator, so I carried it from the auditorium to the kitchen sink. After washing the bottle and putting it into the refrigerator, I turned to return to the auditorium and was surprised at what I saw. Every few inches, there was a drop of soy sauce. I quickly wiped it up and prayed that the smell would be gone by Sunday.

When I saw the trail of soy sauce that I had left behind me, I remembered these words in Revelation 14:13: "Their works do follow them." When we are called home to be with the Lord, we leave behind a trail of works, so like the apostle Paul, let's leave a good example for those who come after us. "For yourselves know how ye ought to follow us: for we behaved not ourselves disorderly among you" (Second Thessalonians 3:7 and 9)

Parents especially should give serious consideration to the example they leave behind. Even if we encourage our children to "follow after righteousness, godliness, faith, love, patience, meekness" (First Timothy 6:11), if we, through our actions, attitude, and words do not leave an example for them, they will ignore our words.

I looked behind me and saw a trail of soy sauce. Look behind you. What kind of trail do you see?

A WHITE ISLAND AND A WHITE HEART

Last Sunday Kyushu became a white island. It snowed all the way from Kitakyushu to Kagoshima. Many towns set new records for low temperatures. For several days I did not need a refrigerator. Except for one room, the entire house became a refrigerator. For the first time the Sunday services at the Kokura church were cancelled.

I think the snow is beautiful. I enjoy sitting at my window and watching the snow get deeper and deeper. When I was young, the snow was a great delight to me. School would be cancelled. We would build snowmen, have snowball fights and ride on our sleds.

As I watched the snow from my window, I thought of two Bible verses. "Come now, and let us reason together, saith the Lord: though your sins be as scarlet, they shall be as white as snow; though they be red like crimson, they shall be as wool." (Isaiah 1:18)

The other verse is written in Psalm 51. Having committed a horrific sin, David is pleading for God's forgiveness. In verse 7 he prayed, "Wash me, and I shall be whiter than snow."

The Bible teaches that the heart of the person who believes in Jesus Christ, the Savior who died on the cross for our sins, will become white as snow. If you would like for God to wash your heart with the precious blood of Christ that flowed from His body on the cross, pray this prayer:

"Lord Jesus, I long to be perfectly whole; I want Thee forever to live in my soul; Break down every idol, cast out every foe; Now wash me, and I shall be whiter than snow." (from the hymn "Whiter Than Snow")

BABU

Mrs. Akanuma lived with her dog in the town of Miyako in Iwate Prefecture. On the afternoon of March 11, she was resting in her living room when the earthquake happened. Immediately 12-year-old Babu began to bark loudly and run around the room. It was not time for his afternoon walk yet, but she put the leash on him and went outside.

Instead of going in the usual direction of their walk, Babu headed for a hill in the opposite direction. Whenever Mrs. Akanuma slowed down, Babu would look behind at her, as if he were saying, "Hurry! Hurry!" Pulling hard on the leash, Babu pulled her to the top of the hill. When she was finally able to rest on top of the hill, Mrs. Akanuma looked behind her and couldn't believe her eyes. Her house and most of the trail that she had just walked with Babu were being swallowed up by an enormous tidal wave. Babu had saved her life.

According to the Bible, a tidal wave much greater than the tidal wave that destroyed Mrs. Akanuma's house is coming. It is the tidal wave of God's judgment on sin. Many, many passages in the Bible warn us about this judgment. For example, in Hebrews 9:27 it is written, "It is appointed unto men once to die, but after this the judgment"

However, just as there was a savior to save Mrs. Akanuma from the tidal wave, there is a Savior who can save us from the tidal wave of the judgment of God. His name is Jesus Christ. Christ died on the cross for our sins. Every person who believes in Christ will be saved from judgment. "Verily, verily, I say unto you, He that heareth my word, and believeth on him that sent me, hath everlasting life, and shall not come into condemnation; but is passed from death unto life." (John 5:24)

BEAUTIFUL FEET?

I often receive requests from supporting churches. The most common one is, "Please send us a new picture." Another one is, "Please send us the results of your evangelism last year." Sometimes, when the pastor changes, I receive long questionnaires concerning my faith.

One day I received a strange request from a church. They wanted me to send a picture of my feet. The slogan for the church's conference for that year was "Beautiful Feet." The slogan was based on Romans 10:15. "How beautiful are the feet of them that preach the gospel of peace, and bring glad tidings of good things!"

This request was a request that troubled me greatly, for my feet are not beautiful feet at all. They are the feet of a 67-year-old man. On my left foot there is a scar from an operation. My right foot has been slightly deformed from birth and is about two inches shorter than my left foot. The church that requested the picture intended to post the pictures on the wall. Without a doubt, my feet would be the ugliest feet on the wall.

What about you? Do you think your feet are beautiful? Have you ever thought even one time, "How beautiful my feet are!" If not, please know this. According to the Word of God, the feet of those who preach the gospel are beautiful feet.

When the Lord sees us passing out flyers and tracts or telling someone else about Jesus, He says, "Look how beautiful their feet are!"

"How beautiful upon the mountains are the feet of him that bringeth good tidings, that publisheth salvation." (Isaiah 52:7)

"BEEP, BEEP, BEEP"

There is one thing I always do when I travel by plane. Before I go through security, I put my watch, my wallet, my cell phone and all other metallic objects into my briefcase. I do this because I do not want the security machine to go "beep, beep, beep" when I go through it.

However, when I went to Tokyo last month, the machine went "beep, beep, beep." The security guard said, "Take off your shoes and go through again." I protested, "But I put all metallic objects into my briefcase." When I went through, the result was the same. "Beep, beep, beep."

"Take off your overcoat and go through again." "Beep, beep, beep." "Take off your coat and go through again." "Beep, beep, beep." I was starting to wonder how much I would have to take off before I could get through security. Finally, the guard said, "You may go."

Imagine having to go through a security check when we enter the gate of heaven. "Beep, beep, beep." We protest, "But I have lived a good life." "Beep, beep, beep." "But I have been baptized." "Beep, beep, beep." "But I am a church member." "Beep, beep, beep."

God answers our protests with the words written in John 3:3, "Except a man be born again, he cannot see the kingdom of God." No matter how righteous a life a person may live, unless he is born again by God's grace through faith in Jesus Christ, he cannot enter heaven. In John 14:6 Jesus said, "No man cometh unto the Father, but by me." To avoid hearing "beep, beep, beep," we must take off our good works and baptism and church membership and enter through faith in Christ alone.

BEWARE OF THE WOLVES

In the ghost stories of Japan there is a story about a wolf that causes people to shudder. According to the story, there is a wolf that follows people who walk on lonely roads in the mountains or country at night. When the person who is walking there hears footsteps behind them, he stops, but the footsteps stop too. At that time the person must walk carefully, for if he stumbles, he will be torn into pieces by the wolf.

A long time ago there were wolves in Honshu, Shikoku, and Kyushu. However, it is believed that the last wolf in Japan was killed in Wakayama Prefecture in 1905, so the wolf has become extinct in Japan.

Japanese wolves may no longer exist, but wolves who try to deceive Christians still exist. In Matthew 7:15 Christ said, "Beware of false prophets, which come to you in sheep's clothing, but inwardly they are ravening wolves."

Paul wrote about these wolves in Acts 20:29. "For I know this, that after my departing shall grievous wolves enter in among you, not sparing the flock."

The characteristics of the wolves who attack the faith of Christians are explained in Romans 16:17- 18. "Mark them which cause divisions and offences contrary to the doctrine which ye have learned; and avoid them. For they that are such serve not our Lord Jesus Christ, but their own belly; and by good words and fair speeches deceive the hearts of the simple."

Beware of the wolves.

"BLUE CAR" CHRISTIANS

The color of most cars in Japan is either white, black, or silver. Until recently, both my van and my small car were those two colors. Whenever I went shopping, I would use the small black car. Many times, after shopping, I have tried to get into someone else's car, for there were several cars in the parking lot that were identical to mine.

Last week I got rid of the black car and bought a pretty blue car. When I went shopping the other day, I was able to find my car right away. It was the only blue car in a parking lot full of black, white, and silver cars.

A Christian should be like one blue car in a parking lot filled with black, white, and silver cars. In other words, the holy lifestyle of the Christian should stand out in a sinful society. The Christian whose attitude, actions and words are different from those of people who do not follow Christ will stand out in a crowd of people.

Of course, in order to stand out, our characteristics will have to be the same as those that are called "the fruit of the Spirit." "The fruit of the Spirit is love, joy, peace, longsuffering, gentleness, goodness, faith, meekness, temperance." (Galatians 5:22:23) When these characteristics are visible in us, we will stand out among the people around us, and we will be given opportunities to witness of our faith in Christ to the people who notice. Like Peter and John in chapter four of Acts, people will notice that "we have been with Jesus."

Hiding our faith is not an option. Let's be "blue car Christians" who are not afraid to stand up for Jesus Christ and let our lives shine forth the glory of God. (Matthew 5:16)

CAN YOU IMAGINE JAPAN WITH NO CHERRY BLOSSOM TREES?

In 2012 many cherry blossom trees in Akita Prefecture began to die. An expert who studied the problem discovered that the cause was an insect called a red-necked longhorn beetle. This species of beetle is not native to Japan. It is thought that the red-necked longhorn beetle entered Japan through packages from overseas.

Normally, beetles lay about 200 eggs, but the red-necked longhorn beetle can lay more than 500 eggs. Also, this beetle can travel more than a mile by riding the wind. Since 2012, this beetle has spread to eleven other prefectures. According to Professor Ryutaro Iwata of Nihon University, if a method to stop this beetle is not found, 30 years from now, there will be no more cherry blossom trees in Japan.

Like the red-necked longhorn beetle that destroys a tree by eating it from the inside, the sins that defile a man are sins that defile him from the inside of his heart. In Mark 7:20-23 Christ said, "That which cometh out of the man, that defileth the man. For from within, out of the heart of men, proceed evil thoughts, adulteries, fornications, murders, Thefts, covetousness, wickedness deceit, lasciviousness, an evil eye, blasphemy, pride, foolishness: All these evil things come from within, and defile the man."

Because the sins that defile a man come out of his heart, we need a new heart. According to Second Corinthians 5:17, God will give a new heart to anyone who will believe in Jesus Christ. "Therefore if any man be in Christ, he is a new creature: old things are passed away; behold, all things are become new."

CATCH PHRASES FOR THE CHRISTIAN LIFE

When I arrived in Japan in 1968, I soon became a fan of sumo. During these many years that I have watched sumo, the most powerful grand champion I ever saw was Taiho who passed away last week. To this day, he holds many sumo records.

He was quite popular with the children. In fact, he was so popular there was a catch phrase for things children liked the most – "Taiho, the Giants, fried eggs." When I read this in the newspaper, I asked myself, "What would be a good catch phrase for the Christian life?"

Because I am a missionary, the first one that came to mind is found in Matthew 28:19-20. "Go ye therefore, and teach all nations, baptizing them in the name of the Father, and of the Son, and of the Holy Ghost: Teaching them to observe all things whatsoever I have commanded you: and, lo, I am with you always, even unto the end of the world. Amen." A wonderful catch phrase for the Christian life would be "Go, Make, Teach."

Of course, the catch phrase written in First Corinthians 13:13 would be an excellent catch phrase – "Faith, Hope, Love."

A catch phrase easy to remember is found in John 14:6. "Jesus saith unto him, I am the way, the truth, and the life: no man cometh unto the Father, but by me." "Way, Truth, Life."

Let me suggest one more that comes from Ephesians 2:4-5 – "Mercy, Love, Grace." What a great catch phrase that honors the Lord who helps Christians who are trying daily to live a life that is pleasing to Him.

CHERRY BLOSSOM SHRIMP

When I went to preach at the Shimizu Bible Baptist Church, Pastor Michishita took me to Nihondaira. From the restaurant we could see Mount Fuji. There was "cherry blossom shrimp ramen" on the menu, so I ordered it. Both the ramen and the shrimp were delicious. The shrimp is the color of the cherry blossom, so it is called "cherry blossom shrimp."

Pastor Michishita told me this story, The deepest bay in Japan is Suruga Bay. One day a fisherman fishing in Suruga Bay accidentally let his net down deeper than usual. The fish that he caught that day was the cherry blossom shrimp.

When I heard this story, I was reminded of the incident recorded in chapter five of Luke. "He entered into one of the ships, which was Simon's, and prayed him that he would thrust out a little from the land. And he sat down, and taught the people out of the ship. Now when he had left speaking, he said unto Simon, 'Launch out into the deep, and let down your nets for a draught.' And Simon answering said unto him, 'Master, we have toiled all the night, and have taken nothing: nevertheless at thy word I will let down the net.' And when they had this done, they inclosed a great multitude of fishes: and their net brake."

"Launch out into the deep." If we are still wading in the shallow water of faith, let's obey the Lord's command and go out deeper, perhaps as deep as baptism or church membership or surrender for full-time ministry.

The delicious cherry blossom shrimp is found in the deep waters of Suruga Bay. Likewise, the most wonderful blessings of the Christian life are found when we launch out into the deep.

CHICKEN SOUP

One Monday last month I was supposed to go to Tottori with Pastor Miyake and his wife; however, three days earlier I had caught a cold. When I woke up on Monday, I knew right away that I would not be able to go with them. I called him, canceled the trip, took some medicine, and went back to bed.

When I awoke, there was a message from Pastor Miyake on my answering machine. "My wife heard that if you eat chicken soup when you have a cold, you will get better. She made you some chicken soup and I took it to your house, but you were asleep, so I left it on the porch." I opened the front door and found the soup. It was still warm, so I ate some right away.

The belief that chicken soup will cure a cold is called an "old wives' tale" that is considered a superstition by most people. However, scientists have researched this superstition and discovered that there are properties in chicken soup that suppress inflammation. They also learned that the warm soup helps the throat, and the steam rising from the soup is helpful in opening the sinuses.

Although the chicken soup did not cure my cold, it was quite delicious. The kindness of Mrs. Miyake who made the soup and Pastor Miyake who brought the soup to my house made it even more delicious.

It is easy to say, 'I love you,' but kind deeds are the proof of our love. At the end of the famous parable about the Good Samaritan, Jesus said, "Go and do thou likewise." We say that we love others but is there any "chicken soup" that proves our love?

CHRIST WAS RAISED IN
THE THIRD MONTH?

We had planned some special services for Easter Sunday. With the help of one of the church members, I prepared a flyer, took it to the printer and had 3000 flyers printed. When I picked up the flyers and took them back to church, one of the men looked at them and said, "Pastor, this is terrible! According to this flyer, Jesus was raised not on the third day but in the third month."

I looked at the flyer. In place of the Chinese character for "day", the character for "month" was written. (The two characters are very similar. There is just one little line on the bottom of the character for "month" that makes it different from "day.") I took the flyers back to the printer and showed him the mistake. He took out the copy I had given to him and showed it to me. Sure enough, instead of the character for "day", there was the character for "month." Knowing nothing about Christianity, the printer printed them that way.

We did not have enough money to throw the flyers away and have new ones printed, so I hurriedly contacted the church members. They gathered at church and corrected all 3000 of the flyers by hand.

Now and then we can see mistakes like this in the writings of men, but we cannot find one mistake in the Word of God. The Bible is a perfect book without one error or contradiction. "The words of the Lord are pure words." (Psalm 12:6) "The law of the Lord is perfect." (Psalm 19:7) "Every word of God is pure." (Proverbs 30:5)

There is not one jot or tittle in the Bible that cannot be trusted, so with assurance, the Christian can live a life based on the Word of God.

DELICIOUS GRAPES
AND A SORE BACK

Last Sunday the believers of the Kokura church and the Kitakyushu church went to a vineyard together to pick grapes. It was the first time for me. I tried to imagine what the vineyard would look like, but when I arrived there, I was surprised, for it was much different than I had imagined. I was especially surprised at the height of the vineyard. Most of the trees were shorter than I am.

The vineyard was so low that I had to bend over to avoid hitting my head on the branches, I laughingly said to a nearby friend, "You have to be humble to pick grapes." I was in the vineyard only about fifteen minutes, but when I left the vineyard, my back was hurting. However, as I enjoyed the delicious grapes for the next few days, I was glad I endured the back pain.

Just as I had to humble myself to gather the delicious grapes, we have to humble ourselves to obtain blessings from the Lord. If we will do so, we shall be able to enjoy many "delicious" blessings.

"A man's pride shall bring him low: but honour shall uphold the humble in spirit." (Proverbs 29:23)

"God resisteth the proud, but giveth grace unto the humble." (James 4:6)

"Humble yourselves in the sight of the Lord, and he shall lift you up." (James 4:10)

There are many wonderful blessings like this in the vineyard of the Lord that can be obtained by the person who is willing to humble himself.

DELIVERED FROM DEATH ROW

Imagine this situation. Although you are innocent, you are found guilty of murder and sentenced to die. Imagine your life in prison. Each morning when you wake up on death row, this thought comes to your mind: "Will it be today? Will I be put to death today? Today I may be executed for a crime I did not commit." Imagine living like this day after day for 48 years!

The headline of the newspaper on March 28th was DEATH SENTENCE REVOKED; FREED AFTER 48 YEARS ON DEATH ROW. On the basis of new DNA evidence, 78-year-old Iwao Hakamada, who entered prison at the age of 30, was freed from death row. Imagine his life as he no longer has to fear execution.

You may be shocked when you read this but, according to the Bible, we have all received a death sentence. In Romans 5:12 it is written, "Wherefore, as by one man sin entered into the world, and death by sin; and so death passed upon all men, for that all have sinned:"

The fact that all people are sinners cannot be denied. Furthermore, the Bible teaches that all sinners will be judged and receive a death sentence. "For the wages of sin is death." (Romans 6:23)

However, we too can be delivered from this sentence of death, not because, like Mr. Hakamada, we are innocent but because Jesus Christ died on the cross and received the punishment for our sins in our place. "Who his own self bare our sins in his own body on the tree." (First Peter 2:24) We do not have to live a life of fear on death row. Personal faith in Jesus Christ will set us free.

KEN BOARD

DEMON SLAYER

Have you heard of the comic book called "Demon Slayer?" It is a story about a boy named Tanjiro. His family was killed by a demon and his sister was turned into a demon, so he became a Demon Slayer to rescue his sister and change her back into a human being.

This comic appeared in the magazine *Shoonen Jump* and then became a TV cartoon. It has been translated into English too. As of December 2020, the comic had over 120 million copies in circulation. It is estimated to have generated total sales of at least $2,700,000,000 in Japan. It is considered to be one of the best anime of this decade.

Of course, this comic is fiction. However, there is a story about a real Demon Slayer that is not fiction. According to First John 3:8, "The Son of God was manifested that he might destroy the works of the devil." God's Son, Jesus Christ, is the real Demon Slayer.

The Bible teaches that the whole world is under the control of Satan. (First John 5:19) In Second Corinthians 4:4 Satan is called "the god of this world." In Ephesians 2:2-3 it is written, "Wherein in time past ye walked according to the course of this world, according to the prince of the power of the air, the spirit that now worketh in the children of disobedience: Among whom also we all had our conversation in times past in the lusts of our flesh, fulfilling the desires of the flesh and of the mind; and were by nature the children of wrath, even as others."

However, when we read chapters 19-20 of Revelation, we learn that our Demon Slayer, the Lord Jesus Christ, will defeat the devil and cast him into the lake of fire and brimstone.

EARTHQUAKE OMENS

Five times a week Mrs. Sachiko Abe wakes up at midnight to see her husband off to his job as a fisherman. One morning when she opened her door at about 1:50, she was surprised by the noise of a flock of crows. Their cry was like a cry that she and her husband had never heard before. Not only that, the number of crows was about three times the usual number.

The same day, from about 10:00 in the morning until noon, Mrs. Yoshiko Sato, who lives near Mrs. Abe, noticed the strange actions of a flock of birds who usually were quiet. They were chirping in a high-pitched tone.

That day was March 11. The strange actions of the crows and the birds were omens of the great earthquake that would occur that day. There are two similar proverbs in Japanese and Chinese. "When a flock of crows move, watch out for an earthquake," and, "When a flock of crows begin to caw with a strange sound, an earthquake is possible."

The Bible speaks of omens before the second coming of Christ. "Great earthquakes shall be in divers places, and famines, and pestilences; and fearful sights and great signs shall there be from heaven." (Luke 21:11)

In verses 25-26 of the same passage, the Bible says, "And there shall be signs in the sun, and in the moon, and in the stars; and upon the earth distress of nations, with perplexity; the sea and the waves roaring; Men's hearts failing them for fear."

The Bible speaks clearly about events like the events of March 11 and the fear of men that will follow these events

ELDERLY DRIVER'S MARK

In April I turned seventy, so I had to put an "elderly driver's mark" on my car. The purpose of this mark is to let other drivers know, "The person who is driving this car is an elderly person who may no longer be a good driver, so be careful."

From 1997 until this year, the elderly driver's mark was in the shape of a leaf. The colors were orange and yellow, so it was called the "maple leaf mark." Because of those colors, it was also called the "withered leaf mark" and the "fallen leaf mark." After protests by the elderly people of Japan, it was changed to the shape of a clover with an S for "Senior" in the middle. The colors were changed to green symbolizing youth and orange and yellow symbolizing knowledge.

Sadly, the lives of many people over seventy resemble a withered or fallen leaf. In Psalm 90:10 Moses summarized the feelings of many elderly people. "The days of our years are threescore years and ten; and if by reason of strength they be fourscore years, yet is their strength labour and sorrow; for it is soon cut off, and we fly away."

Certainly, elderly people have many problems such as poor health and loneliness. Their life is like a withered life waiting for the wind to blow it away. However, the elderly person who believes in Christ does not have to live out his life like a withered or fallen leaf. Titus 2:2-3 encourages the elderly to "be sound in faith, charity and patience," to "be in behavior as becometh holiness," and to be "teachers of good things."

We who have the "elderly person's mark' on our life must not think that we are like a withered leaf that is no longer of any use to the Lord.

"EVACUATE AS QUICKLY AS YOU CAN!"

On September 3rd typhoon #5 came ashore at the town of Gojo in Nara Prefecture. Mr. Takehara took refuge in the town hall. However, he was worried about the people living near the river in Tsujido, so he left the town hall and went to warn them. He went to 34 homes near the river and warned them. "Evacuate as quickly as possible!" Ninety percent of them were over 65 years of age. Pulling them and pushing them from behind, he was able to evacuate them to the town hall. Shortly thereafter, a landslide destroyed their homes, so his actions saved their lives.

Why did he know they were in danger? In both 1889 and 1953 many people in Tsujido had lost their lives in a typhoon. Mr. Takehara's parents told him about those disasters and warned him repeatedly to flee if a typhoon came. He said, "The information we learned from past typhoons was a great help."

An Englishman named Edmund Burke once said, "Those who don't know history are destined to repeat it."

The Bible teaches the same principle. In First Corinthians 10:7-10 there is a list of the sins that the people of Israel committed, and then in verses 11-12 it is written, "Now all these things happened unto them for examples: and they are written for our admonition, upon whom the ends of the world are come. Wherefore let him that thinketh he standeth take heed lest he fall."

The purpose of the interesting stories of the Old Testament is not just to entertain us. They were written to protect us from the landslides of sin, so we must not ignore their warnings.

EVEN THOUGH THE
MOUNTAINS SHAKE

This week I preached at a missions conference at the Chofu Baptist Temple. After having dinner on Thursday night with Pastor Ishikawa, I returned to my hotel room. About nine o'clock there was a call from Assistant Pastor Tokoro. He asked, "Are you watching television right now? If not, turn on the TV. There was an earthquake in Kyushu."

For the next two hours I watched the broadcast from Kumamoto City. I have lived in Kyushu for 48 years. During that time there have been powerful typhoons and volcanic eruptions but never a natural disaster on this scale. I immediately called my son in Kyushu. He and his family were safe. I called several churches. There was no damage to any of them.

As I watched the broadcast of the destruction in Kumamoto City, right away two Bible passages came to my mind. The first one was a prophecy written in Revelation 16:18. "And there were voices, and thunders, and lightnings; and there was a great earthquake, such as was not since men were upon the earth, so mighty an earthquake, and so great." It will be an earthquake greater than any earthquake that has ever taken place in Japan.

The other passage was Psalm 46:1-3. "God is our refuge and strength, a very present help in trouble. "Therefore will not we fear, …though the mountains shake with the swelling thereof. Selah."

Even though we become Christians through faith in Christ, there may be sudden "earthquakes" that take place in our lives; however, when those sudden trials come, let us remember that the Lord is our refuge and strength, so there is no need to fear.

EVERY DAY IS HEAVEN

On the island of Kyushu there is an interesting place called "Hell." It is divided into seven Hells consisting of hot springs and boiling mud. The water in some of the springs is over 200 degrees.

At the entrance to each spring there is a store that sells souvenirs. Every time I go there, there is one thing that catches my eye. It is a t-shirt. These words are written in Japanese on the shirt – "Every day is Hell."

There might be people who say, "It is true. Every day is hell." However, the person who believes in Christ can say the opposite. In other words, "Every day is heaven." If we look at Psalm 23, we understand why the Christian can say, "Every day is heaven."

"The Lord is my shepherd; I shall not want. He maketh me to lie down in green pastures: he leadeth me beside the still waters. He restoreth my soul: he leadeth me in the paths of righteousness for his name's sake." The Lord makes us sufficient in all things, He gives rest and peace to our soul, and He restores us and leads us in the right path, so every day is heaven.

"Yea, though I walk through the valley of the shadow of death, I will fear no evil: for thou art with me; thy rod and thy staff they comfort me. Thou preparest a table before me in the presence of mine enemies: thou anointest my head with oil; my cup runneth over. Surely goodness and mercy shall follow me all the days of my life: and I will dwell in the house of the Lord for ever." The Lord delivers us from fear and comforts us. He gives us overflowing joy, and He protects us with His goodness and mercy, so every day is heaven.

"FILL IT UP"

Usually, when I drive to see my son and his family in Kagoshima, I fill the car with gas before I leave, but I already had half a tank, so I thought, "If I wait and fill it up on the way, I will not have to get gas on the way home." I drove as far as the Miyahara service area, pulled into a stand and said to the attendant, "Fill it up."

About fifteen minutes down the road, I looked at my gas gauge and was surprised. It was not even three-fourths full. I had clearly told the attendant, "Fill it up," but he did not even put in three-fourths, so I had to stop and get gas again on the way home.

"Fill it up." These words are spoken by many people to the things of this world. They want sports, pleasure, wine, religion, wealth, work or education to fill the emptiness in their hearts. The words of Solomon in chapter two of Ecclesiastes echo their futile attempts to be fulfilled.

"I said in mine heart, Go to now, I will prove thee with mirth, therefore enjoy pleasure: and, behold, this also is vanity." (verse 1) "And whatsoever mine eyes desired I kept not from them, I withheld not my heart from any joy; for my heart rejoiced in all my labour: and this was my portion of all my labour. Then I looked on all the works that my hands had wrought, and on the labour that I had laboured to do: and, behold, all was vanity and vexation of spirit, and there was no profit under the sun." (verses 10-11}

True fulfillment comes to the person who puts his trust in the Lord. "He satisfieth the longing soul, and filleth the hungry soul with goodness." (Psalm 107:9)

FIVE LITERS OF MILK EVERY DAY!

Last Sunday the Sumo Association held a ceremony to introduce the twelve young men who had passed the test to become new sumo wrestlers. One young man was six feet two inches tall and weighed 271 pounds. There are many sumo wrestlers this big, so his height and weight are not unusual. The unusual thing is his age. He is only fifteen years old.

How did he grow to six feet two inches and 271 pounds by the age of fifteen? He decided to strengthen his body by drinking milk. He drank five liters (1.3 gallons) every day!

He is a good example to all Christians. We should drink milk every day to become a strong Christian. Of course, I am not talking about the milk we buy at the store. I am talking about the milk of the Word of God. In First Peter 2:2 we are exhorted to "desire the sincere milk of the word, that ye may grow thereby." The pure milk of the Word of God is an absolute necessity to spiritual growth and a strong faith.

If we want to be a *makushita* (third division) Christian, let's drink five verses of the milk of the Bible every day. If we want to be a *juuryou* (second division) Christian, let's drink five pages of the milk of God's Word every day. If we want to be a *yokozuna* (grand champion) Christian, let's drink five chapters of the milk of the Bible every day.

In Psalm 119:28 David prayed, "Strengthen thou me according unto thy word." To become a strong Christian, let's pray this prayer and then open the Bible and drink the milk of the Word. After all, our adversary is not a sumo wrestler but "the rulers of the darkness of this world and spiritual wickedness in high places." (Ephesians 6:12)

FORGOTTEN

Since 2011, as soon as the month of March begins, I remember the earthquake and tidal wave that caused unfathomable damage in the Toohoku area. 15,884 people lost their lives. 2,633 people are still missing. Many of the people who evacuated the area may never be able to return to their homes.

I shudder every time I watch the video of the event. When I consider the feelings of the people who could not even imagine a tidal wave that big, I sense a deep sorrow in my heart. I would like to ask the survivors, "Three years have passed since the disaster. What is the worst thing about your experience?" I read the reply of one survivor in a newspaper article. He said, "The worst thing is to be forgotten."

Yes, being forgotten is one of the worst experiences. Much of the content of chapter 19 of the book of Job is the lament of Job. The words that stand out in that lament are these words in verse 14. "My kinsfolk have failed, and my familiar friends have forgotten me."

Perhaps you are going through the same experience right now. A parent or a child, maybe a sibling or a friend has forgotten you and has not contacted you in years.

Parents, children or friends may forget us, but the Lord will never forget the person who believes in Him. One day, the people of Israel said, "The Lord hath forsaken me, and my Lord hath forgotten me." The Lord answered, "Can a woman forget her sucking child, that she should not have compassion on the son of her womb? yea, they may forget, <u>yet will I not forget thee</u>." (Isaiah 49:15)

GETTING A NEW PASSPORT
IS NOT EASY

I had to renew my American passport, so I mailed my old passport, a picture, the renewal application and a $110 check to the American consulate in Fukuoka. A week later, I received a letter from the consulate. "You sent a $110 check, but we do not accept personal checks. Please send cash. Also, the size of your picture is not correct, so send a new picture." I sent the cash and a new picture,

A few days later, I received a phone call from the consulate. "The size of the picture is okay, but we need a picture with a better closeup of your face." I sent a new picture and received my new passport a few days later.

Until I met all the requirements of the consulate, I was not able to receive my new passport. Likewise, until we meet all the requirements of the Lord, we can never receive a new heart. What is it that God requires? It is keeping the famous Ten Commandments written in chapter twenty of Exodus. However, when we try to keep them, we become aware of a terrible truth. We cannot keep them perfectly. According to James 2:10, "For whosoever shall keep the whole law, and yet offend in one point, he is guilty of all."

If keeping the Ten Commandments perfectly is impossible, why did God give them to us? According to Galatians 3:24, the purpose of the commandments is to show us our need of a Savior. "The law was our schoolmaster to bring us unto Christ, that we might be justified by faith."

Receiving a new passport is not easy, but we can easily receive a new heart through faith in Jesus Christ. "Ye are all the children of God by faith in Christ Jesus." (Galatians 3:26)

GETTING THE RUN AROUND

I have to renew my visa on September 1st, so I went to the immigration office and receive the renewal application forms. After filling out the forms and gathering the other necessary documents, I went back to the immigration office.

"You need proof that you paid your taxes, so go to the Kokura ward office and get that document." When I went to the Kokura ward office, I was told, "On January 1st of this year you were still living in Yahata ward, so you must go to the Yahata ward office."

When I went to the Yahata ward office, I was told, "We can't have the document ready today. Come back tomorrow." I was busy the next two days, so three days later I went back to the office again.

Imagine getting run around like this when we arrive at the entrance to heaven. "In order to enter heaven, you need to go back to earth and bring a document proving that you were a church member," or "in order to enter heaven, you need a baptismal certificate."

Let us be thankful that we do not need any documents like that to go to heaven. The one condition to enter heaven is to believe in Jesus Christ and be cleansed by the blood He shed for us on the cross.

In Matthew 5: it is written, "Blessed are the pure in heart: for they shall see God." In Psalm 24:3 there is this question, "Who shall ascend into the hill of the Lord? or who shall stand in his holy place?" The answer is in verse 4. "He that hath clean hands, and a pure heart." A pure heart cleansed by the blood of Christ can get anyone into heaven.

GIFTS FROM OKINAWA

When I heard the doorbell ring, I opened the door and saw a Yamato deliveryman holding a large box. I didn't remember ordering anything that large, so I was quite surprised. When I looked at the label on the box, I realized that it was a package from the Okinawa Bible Baptist Church, a church where I had preached recently.

When I opened the box, I was surprised again. There were many things in the box – cookies, root beer, popcorn, soup, muffins, beef stew, canned goods, nachos, curry, bread and crackers.

When I saw the contents of the box, I rejoiced greatly. This week four Americans will stay at my home, so I needed to buy food, snacks, and drinks. Because of the gifts from the Okinawa church, I will not need to buy very much.

As I took each item out of the box, I remembered the words of Christ in the sermon that He preached on the mountain. "Therefore take no thought, saying, What shall we eat? or, What shall we drink? or, Wherewithal shall we be clothed? (For after all these things do the Gentiles seek:) for your heavenly Father knoweth that ye have need of all these things." (Matthew 6:31-32) God already knew what I needed, so He provided it through the Okinawa church.

God already knows what we need, so there is no need for us to worry. If we obey the commandment in Matthew 6:33, we can be assured that God knows our needs and will supply them. "But seek ye first the kingdom of God, and his righteousness; and all these things shall be added unto you."

GO BACK TO GO FORWARD

When I went to the Ueda Bible Baptist Church in Ueda City in Nagano Prefecture, I rode the Bullet train from Kokura to Tokyo and then from Tokyo to Nagano. The train on which I was riding did not stop at Ueda, so I had to change to a different train that stopped at stations where the Bullet train does not stop.

When I boarded that local train, I noticed something interesting. That train was bound for Tokyo. Even though I had just come from Tokyo, in order to go to Ueda City, I had to ride a train headed back to Tokyo.

There are times when Christians too must go back to go forward. When we realize that our life is no longer pleasing to the Lord, we may have to go back to the place where we did not obey the will of God and repent.

In chapter 28 of Genesis, Jacob, who had stolen the blessings of his brother Esau and feared being killed by him, fled to a place called Bethel. There he made a vow to God, but after he arrived in Haram, he forgot his vow and lived a very sinful life.

Twenty years later, Jacob went back to Bethel, built an altar, and renewed his vows to God. (Genesis 35:1-15)

The Christian who wants to be more blessed by God or grow more spiritually or be more useful to the Lord may have to first go back to the place where he did not keep his promise to God and renew his decision to obey the Lord. It is only when we go back to our own Bethel and make things right with the Lord that we shall be able to experience the fullness of the blessings that God has for us.

"GOCHISOOSAMA DESHITA"

Last Monday I went to an all-you-can-eat Korean barbecue restaurant with a friend. We both ate a lot of delicious meat and vegetables. I intended to pay for the meal, but when I went to the register to pay, I learned that he had already paid. I said to him, *"Gochisoosama deshita."* (Thank you for the delicious meal.)

The next day, I went to a restaurant called "Ringer Hut" with another friend. I ate some delicious *champon* (a noodle and vegetable dish) and the g*yoza* (meat dumplings) that I love. Again, I intended to pay for the meal, but my friend insisted on paying. I said to him too, *"Gochisoosama deshita."*

Both times I intended to pay, but my friends paid for me. As I was thinking about that on the way home, the words of the hymn *Jesus Paid It All* came to my mind. This hymn was written by a lady named Elvina Hall. One Sunday, during her pastor's long sermon, she began to meditate on the price that Christ paid for our salvation.

These are the words that she wrote that day: "Jesus paid it all, all to Him I owe; Sin had left a crimson stain, He washed it white as snow."

I said, "Thank you for the delicious meal," to my friends who paid for my meals. To my Savior, Jesus Christ, who paid the price of my salvation with His own precious blood, I want to say, "Thank you for your wonderful salvation."

"There is one God, and one mediator between God and men, the man Christ Jesus; Who gave himself a ransom for all." (First Timothy 2:6)

KEN BOARD

GOLDEN WEEK ISN'T VERY GOLDEN

The period from April 29th to March 5th is called Golden Week. I do not know who named it Golden Week, but I think it is a person who never made a trip by car during that period.

Last year, during Golden Week, Pastor Miyake and I took several young people to a Camp in the Kansai area. We left about dusk and drove to the Faith Baptist Church in Iwakuni and spent the night there. The next morning, we headed for Camp. A trip that should have taken six hours took twelve hours!

This year I headed for Kagoshima Prefecture during Golden Week to preach at the Grace Baptist Church in Nagashima. A trip that should have taken five hours took seven and a half hours!

There are three meanings of "golden" in the English language – the color gold, radiant, and splendid or perfect. The person who thought of the name "Golden Week" probably was thinking of the third of those meanings – splendid or perfect; however, to people who have to make a trip by car at that time. Golden Week isn't very golden.

Believers in Christ will one day see something that is truly golden – gold in color, brilliant and splendid. According to Revelation 21:18, the city that God has prepared for us is "pure gold like unto clear glass."

There is one other golden thing found in the Bible. It is called the "golden rule." In Matthew 7:12 Jesus said, "All things whatsoever ye would that men should do to you, do ye even so to them:" If we would follow this rule, every week could be a "Golden Week."

GOD'S NUMBER EIGHTEEN

Although I have been living in Japan for 45 years, the other day when I was watching television, I heard an expression that I had never heard before. It was the expression "his number eighteen." I thought about it for a while but could not understand the meaning of the expression. I thought perhaps it had something to do with hole number eighteen in golf. When I asked several Japanese about it, they explained that it is an expression from the world of *kabuki*. It means "his specialty."

When I heard this explanation, I immediately began thinking, "What is God's number eighteen?" Of course, God's number eighteen is doing the impossible. There are several Bible passages that teach this truth. "But Jesus beheld them, and said unto them, "With men this is impossible; but with God all things are possible." (Matthew 19:26) We can see the same truth expressed in Mark 10:27 and Luke 1:37.

God's number eighteen is something man cannot do. For example, if he has the necessary materials, man can build magnificent buildings; however, he cannot make something out of nothing. According to the Bible, God created all things out of nothing just by the power of His words. "By the word of the Lord were the heavens made; and all the host of them by the breath of his mouth." (Psalm 33:6)

When we read the gospels, we see God's number eighteen demonstrated by the power of Christ who healed the sick, walked on the water, and stilled the storm.

When we are placed in seemingly impossible situations, let's seek the help of the Lord. That's His specialty.

GOD'S THUMB

When I went to the Nagashima church last month, I had a new experience -- a full-body massage. When I go to the barber shop, the barber massages my back with a machine, but this was a massage from the top of my head to the bottom of my foot.

There is a man in the Nagashima church who is a masseur. When he asked me, "How about a massage?" I hesitated. To tell the truth, I did not want a massage. However, when I considered the feelings of the brother who wanted to serve me by giving me a massage, I agree to let him give me a massage. During the massage, I cried out in pain several times, especially when his thumb pressed down hard on my muscles; however, after the massage, I felt much better.

There are times when the thumb of the Lord presses down hard on my heart just as the brother in Nagashima pressed down hard on my muscles. When my attitude or actions are not pleasing to Him, the hand of the Lord applies pressure to my heart.

David expressed this experience with these words in Psalm 32:3-4. "When I kept silence, my bones waxed old through my roaring all the day long. For day and night thy hand was heavy upon me: my moisture is turned into the drought of summer."

When the hand of the Lord is pressing heavy upon us because of some action that is not pleasing to the Lord, let us follow the example of David. "I acknowledge my sin unto thee, and mine iniquity have I not hid. I said, I will confess my transgressions unto the Lord; and thou forgavest the iniquity of my sin." (Psalm 32:5)

"GOMA O SURU"

I teach English to several students on Friday. Sometimes, they become the teacher and I become the student. In other words, they teach me Japanese. Recently, they taught me an interesting expression – *goma o suru*. (The word *goma* means "sesame seed.") When they use this expression, they hold one hand over the other and make a grinding motion with the top hand as if they are grinding sesame seeds.

The meaning of this phrase is "to flatter." I could not understand why this phrase meant "to flatter", so I checked the Internet and found this explanation: When they grind the sesame seeds, sesame oil will be pressed out and stick to the grinder here and there. Over the years, this image of the sesame seed oil clinging to the grinder came to mean a person who uses flattery to cling to another person.

The phrase that Americans use to describe a flatterer is not "sesame seed" but "butter." To "butter up" another person is to speak flattering words to them. In Psalm 55:21 David said this about the man who betrayed him: "The words of his mouth were smoother than butter, but war was in his heart: his words were softer than oil."

In Proverbs 29:5 it is written, "A man that flattereth his neighbour spreadeth a net for his feet." Also, Proverbs 28:23 teaches us that, "He that rebuketh a man afterwards shall find more favour than he that flattereth with the tongue."

Flattery might be helpful to maintain a peaceful relationship with another person, but we must be careful that flattery does not become a lie that is used to deceive someone else.

HALF-AND-HALF FAITH

The lady at the front desk of the hotel in Okinawa asked me a question about church. After a short explanation, I asked her, "Have you ever been to church?" This is the conversation that followed:

Lady: "My son goes to a Christian school, so I have attended some services there."

Me: "Are you a Christian?"

Lady: "I have a Buddhist altar in my home, so I am half-and-half."

Me: "Half-and-half won't get you to heaven."

According to the Bible, the person who has half-and-half faith does not have true faith for the Bible clearly teaches that there is only one person who can save us. That person is Jesus Christ who died on the cross for our sins.

In John 14:6 Jesus said, "I am the way, the truth, and the life: no man cometh unto the Father, but by me." In Acts 4:12 it is written, "Neither is there salvation in any other: for there is none other name under heaven given among men, whereby we must be saved."

To rely on Christ plus someone else or something else is half-and-half faith. For example, Christ plus Buddha, Christ plus Mary, Christ plus baptism, Christ plus church membership, or Christ plus good works. To receive forgiveness of sins and receive the privilege to go to heaven, our faith must be faith in Christ and Christ alone.

HAPPY WORDS

When I went shopping at the grocery store, I met a lady that I had not seen for a while. She said, "Pastor Board, you have lost weight, haven't you?" Her words made me very happy.

A couple of days later, I went to the cleaners. The lady said, "You have lost weight, haven't you?" Again, her words made me very happy.

That same week the students of my Friday English class said, "You have lost weight, haven't you?" Three times in one week someone said to me, "You have lost weight, haven't you?" I was extremely happy!

Words like "you have lost weight, haven't you?" make us very happy. For example, when we participate in a game or a contest and win, the word "congratulations" makes us happy. Also, when our parents or children say to us, "I love you," our feeling is a happy feeling.

What are the words that make you happy? Perhaps they are, "Yes, I will marry you," or "You have won the lottery," or "You are now cancer-free." The words that bring me the greatest happiness are the words in John 3:16. "For God so loved the world, that he gave his only begotten Son, that whosoever believeth in him should not perish, but have everlasting life."

Doomed to eternal punishment in Hell and having no power to save ourselves, we were saved by a merciful God who sent His own Son to die on the cross and receive the judgment for sin as our substitute. Do any words exist that can make us happier that the words that promise eternal life to all those who believe in Christ?

HARD PILLOWS

When I arrived in Japan in 1968, there were many things that amazed me. One was the hard pillows. The first time I slept on a Japanese pillow, I felt like I was sleeping on a brick. As I lay there tossing and turning, I remembered the experience of Jacob. "He took of the stones of that place, and put them for his pillows, and lay down in that place to sleep." (Genesis 28:11)

I do not like small, hard pillows. I like soft, fluffy pillows. Every night I sleep on two fluffy pillows.

When I go on a trip, I take my pillow with me. Last month I went to my son's home. As I got out of my car, my grandchildren came running to greet me. Their first words were, "Grandpa, did you bring your pillow?" When I heard their question, I realized that I had forgotten my pillow. I had to sleep on a small, thin pillow while I was there. Next time, I will be sure to take my pillow.

What kind of pillow was the pillow of Christ? Have you ever thought about that? It appears that He did not have a pillow. In Luke 9:58 Jesus said, "Foxes have holes, and birds of the air have nests; but the Son of man hath not where to lay his head."

Not only did Jesus not have a pillow, He did not have a place to put His pillow. Tonight, whether you sleep on a fluffy pillow like my pillow or a hard pillow like the pillows of Japan, ponder these words. "For ye know the grace of our Lord Jesus Christ, that, though he was rich, yet for your sakes he became poor, that ye through his poverty might be rich." (Second Corinthians 8:9)

HE CUT THE BALL IN HALF!

Have you seen the video of Isao Machii on You Tube? Since the video was placed on You Tube, it has been viewed by over three million people.

Isao Machii is a swordmaster. On the video he cuts a baseball that was thrown at 100 miles an hour in half! The distance from home plate to the pitcher's mound is sixty feet and sixty inches. The ball that Isao cut in half was thrown from a distance of only thirty feet!

What is the secret of his amazing skill? One secret is his reaction ability developed through years of practice. The other secret is the sharpness of his sword. Imagine the sharpness of a sword that was able to cut in half a baseball thrown at 100 miles an hour from a distance of only thirty feet!

However, I know a sword even sharper than his sword. In Hebrews 4:12 there is an explanation of the amazing sharpness of the Word of God. "The word of God is quick, and powerful, and sharper than any twoedged sword, piercing even to the dividing asunder of soul and spirit, and of the joints and marrow, and is a discerner of the thoughts and intents of the heart."

The Bible we hold in our hands is a sharp sword. In chapter six of Ephesians there is a list of the armor we should put on in order to stand against the wiles of the devil. One piece of that armor is the Bible. "The sword of the Spirit, which is the word of God." (verse 18)

Every Christian should desire to be a swordmaster like Isao Machii. To do that, we have to read our Bible daily, we have to study it at church every week, and we have to store the Word of God in our heart by memorizing many verses.

HE HAD HIS FOOT ON THE BRAKE

I am over seventy now, so I have to go to driving school to renew my driver's license. First, there was a speech and a DVD. Next, there was a test to check our ability to react quickly. We were tested on machines like the ones you would find in a game center. It was fun but also difficult. Finally, we had to drive a real car.

I have confidence in my driving, so I was able to drive through the driving school course skillfully. At one point, we came to a stop sign. I stopped the car and looked to the left and to the right. There was a car coming from the right, but it was coming at a very slow speed, so I stepped on the accelerator and tried to go, but the car would not move. I stepped on the gas again, but the car did not move. The driving instructor said to me, "I have my foot on the brake, so the car is not going to move." I thought I had plenty of room to beat the other car, but the instructor thought my judgment was mistaken, so he put his foot on the brake. (I told him later, "I could have beaten that car." He just laughed,)

There are times when God does a similar thing. A Christian tries to go forward on the path he has chosen, but that path is not the will of God, so He puts His foot on the brake and will not let the Christian go that way. In Psalm 37:23 it is written, "The steps of a good man are ordered by the LORD." I heard a preacher say, "The stops as well as the steps are ordered by the Lord." When we just cannot seem to make any progress with our plans, let us stop and consider the possibility that our plan is not the will of God, so He has His foot on the brake.

"A man's heart deviseth his way: but the LORD directeth his steps." (Proverbs 16:9)

HE TRIED TO PAY FOR
HIS DRINK TWICE

Last month a friend stayed at my home. Although he has been living in Japan many years, he had never been to Nagasaki, so I offered to take him there. On the way we stopped at a service area to buy something to drink and some snacks. My friend bought a drink from a vending machine.

As I was searching for a tasty snack, suddenly I noticed a commotion at the store's cash register. When I went to see what was happening, I saw the store clerk with a confused look on her face talking to my friend. When I heard what she was saying, I couldn't help but laugh. Several people standing nearby were laughing too. My friend was trying to pay for the drink that he had already bought from the vending machine. The conversation between him and the girl at the cash register was hilarious.

Many people like my friend who tried to pay for his drink twice are trying to earn a salvation that Jesus already bought for us on the cross. According to Acts 20:28, Jesus has bought our salvation with His own blood. Some people are trying to earn salvation by zealously participating in religious activities. Others are trying to earn salvation by their good works.

In First Peter 1:18-19 it is written, "Forasmuch as ye know that ye were not redeemed with corruptible things, as silver and gold, from your vain conversation received by tradition from your fathers; But with the precious blood of Christ, as of a lamb without blemish and without spot."

Salvation is not something that we earn. It is a gift that God gives to any person who will repent of his sins and believe in Christ.

KEN BOARD

HIDE-AND-SEEK AT THE TRAIN STATION

Last week another missionary and I attended the Pioneer Evangelism Conference in Nagano Prefecture. He would board the train at Hakata and I would board the train later at Kokura. I asked him, "What will you do if I do not get on the train at Kokura?" He replied, "I will get off of the train at the next station and go home."

When the train arrived at Kokura, I hid behind a pole and got on the train at the very last minute. Instead of going to my seat, I hid in the area between the cars. When the train left and I was still not there, my friend came searching for me. When he found me playing hide-and-seek, he laughed.

There may be times when we think God is hiding in some place far away. We may even speak the same words that David spoke. "Why standest thou afar off, O Lord? why 4hidest thou thyself in times of trouble?" (Psalm 10:1) "How long wilt thou forget me, O Lord? for ever? how long wilt thou hide thy face from me?" (Psalm 13:1)

When these words are echoing on our heart, let's remember the promise of God written in Hebrews 13:5. "I will never leave thee, nor forsake thee."

There is one other important thing. Instead of waiting in his seat, my friend came searching for me to see if I were on board the train or not. Likewise, when we begin to doubt whether the Lord is with us or not, let's search for Him through prayer and the Bible. "Ye shall seek me, and find me, when ye shall search for me with all your heart." (Jeremiah 29:13)

HIS BIGGEST OPPONENT

Hakuho won his match on the first day of the Kyushu sumo tournament and extended his winning streak to sixty-three matches in a row. It looked like he might break Futabayama's record of sixty-nine wins in a row, but he lost on the second day of the tournament. Even though he was not able to break the record, sixty-three wins in a row is a remarkable record.

After his 54th win in a row, he was asked in a television interview, "Who is your biggest opponent?" He replied, "My biggest opponent is myself. I am good at technique and I take care of my body, but taking care of my heart is difficult. It is more difficult to defeat my heart than it is to defeat my opponent."

He had learned an important principle that all Christians must learn. Our biggest opponent is ourself. We may blame the failures of our Christian life on others, but the real cause of our failures lies in our own heart.

Consider the experience of David. He was able to defeat the giant, Goliath. After he became king, he was able to conquer his enemies, but when we read chapter eleven of Second Samuel, we see that his inability to conquer his own heart led to terrible moral failures.

In Proverbs 25:28 it is written, "He that hath no rule over his own spirit is like a city that is broken down, and without walls." Paul expressed a similar thought in First Corinthians 9:27. "I keep under my body, and bring it into subjection: lest that by any means, when I have preached to others, I myself should be a castaway." Let's be careful lest we lose the most important battle of all – the battle with our own heart.

HOT TEA

It has been awfully hot later, so I suggested to the church ladies, "During the summer let's have *mugicha* (barley tea) with the meal instead of hot green tea." The next Sunday they prepared barley tea; however, when I drank it, I was disappointed. It was hot barley tea. I had expected cold tea, but because I did not tell the ladies specifically that I wanted cold tea, they prepared hot tea.

We often make the same mistake when we pray. Instead of telling the Lord exactly what we desire, we pray ambiguous prayers full of cliches.

When I moved from Yahata to Kokura, I prayed, "Lord, this is the kind of house I want. First, a house where the rent is about the same as what I pay now. Second, a house with no stairs. Third, a house that already has lights and curtains. Fourth, a house near the church."

The first house the broker showed to me was exactly what I had asked for. The rent was the same as the house in Yahata. There were no stairs. There were lights and curtains in every room. It was a three-minute drive to the church. Not only that, it was much larger and there was room to park both of my cars.

The moment I entered the house, I thought of the words written in Ephesians 3:20. "Now unto him that is able to do exceeding abundantly above all that we ask or think."

Specific prayers bring specific answers. "In every thing by prayer and supplication with thanksgiving let your requests be made known unto God." (Philippians 4:6)

HOW A LOSS BROUGHT
THEM VICTORY

⟶ ❧ ⟵

The Hiroshima Carp are champions of the Central League again this year. Amazingly, among their first eighty-four wins, forty-one of them were come-from-behind victories.

How did the Carp become a team with this come-from-behind ability? This newspaper headline reveals the key to their championship: "Dismay Fostered A Never-Say-Die Spirit." Last year the Carp were defeated in the Japan Series. The dismay in losing the championship led to the never-say-die spirit of this year's team.

The same thing can be said of the life of the Christian. The dismay of trials produces Christians who never give up. According to First Peter 5:10, the mature, strong, unmovable Christian is the Christian who has experienced suffering. "The God of all grace, who hath called us unto his eternal glory by Christ Jesus, <u>after that ye have suffered a while</u>, make you perfect, stablish, strengthen, settle you."

Through trials the Lord raises us strong Christians who will never give up and fight to the finish. Through the trials Christians learn three things: 1-God will keep His promises. 2-We can trust God at all times. 3-God has sufficient power to help us through the trial.

Certainly, trials cause us to dismay. However, the Christian who learns these three truths through trials is the Christian who can live a life of victory.

"In all these things we are more than conquerors through him that loved us." (Romans 8:37)

"HOW FAST ARE YOU GOING?"

"The speed limit here is 80!" (80 km) I yelled these words at a car that passed me at a high speed. Brother and Sister Koh were with me. Brother Koh asked me, "Pastor Board, how fast are you going?" I happened to be going 90 at the time, so I covered the speedometer with my hand so he could not see it. He did not say anything, but I could hear him laughing.

What do you think? Which car committed a speeding violation, the car who passed me at the speed of 110 or my car that was traveling only at the speed of 90? Of course, both cars were going too fast. The speed limit in that area was 80, so any car going over 80 was going too fast. Both cars had committed a speeding violation.

The principle is the same with the laws written in the Bible. The person who commits only a few sins because they are trying to live a good life and the person who commits many sins are both sinners. "For whosoever shall keep the whole law, and yet offend in one point, he is guilty of all." (James 2:10)

Both the person who breaks all of the laws of God and the person who breaks only one of the laws of God have violated His laws. This is the very reason God sent us the Savior, Jesus Christ. Because not one of us is able to keep the laws of God perfectly and save ourself from the judgment of God, we needed a Savior who would die on the cross and receive the judgment of God in our place.

"For he (God) hath made him (Christ) to be sin for us, who knew no sin; that we might be made the righteousness of God in him." (Second Corinthians 5:21)

HOW MANY DAYS ARE LEFT?

Last month I went to Taiwan to visit Brother Sakai, the missionary sent out of the Kokura church. It was a joyous five days. I was greatly blessed by my fellowship with the members of the Peace Bible Baptist Church. There was so much delicious food. I gained several pounds.

Taiwan is a lot like Japan, but there are several differences, especially when it comes to the traffic. In Taiwan, cars drive on the right side of the road. Also, I was amazed at the number of motorbikes. It is said that there are more motorbikes than people in Taiwan. I was also surprised at the number of cars that run red lights.

One more interesting difference was the timers at intersections. The timers show how many seconds are left until the red light turns green.

In the Bible there is a promise that is connected to time. That promise is the second coming of Christ. In John 14:3 Jesus said, "If I go and prepare a place for you, I will come again." When will He come again? According to Matthew 24:36, the Father alone knows the day and hour when Christ will come again.

Do you suppose there is a timer in heaven, a timer that shows how many days and hours are left until Christ comes again? I wonder how many days are left? When we look at the promises of the Bible and the condition of the world, we realize that the days must be few in number. Today, the number of days might be down to one.

If so, we must give heed to the warning in Matthew 24:44. "Be ye also ready: for in such an hour as ye think not the Son of man cometh."

HOW TO DECEIVE A RAZOR CLAM

On the second day of Summer Camp, we went to the beach at Minoshima and spent a delightful time walking in the ocean and collecting shells. Near the place where I was walking, my curiosity was aroused by a man who would open a hole in the sand, pour something into the hole, and then pull something out of the hole.

I asked him, "What are you doing?" He said, "I'm catching razor clams." I asked, "Can I watch?" and he said, "Sure."

He opened a hole in the sand, poured in something, and a razor clam came out. He pulled the clam out of the hole and put it in his bucket. I asked him, "What did you put into the hole?" He replied, "Salt. Right now, it is low tide, but if I put in salt, the clam will think it is high tide and come out of the hole."

I was amazed how easily the razor clam was deceived. Likewise, I am amazed at the number of people who are so easily deceived. Some people are deceived by riches. (Matthew 13:22) They believe that riches will bring them happiness, but in Luke 12:15 Jesus said, "A man's life consisteth not in the abundance of the things which he possesseth."

Other people are deceived by human philosophy. In Colossians 2:8 there is this warning. "Beware lest any man spoil you through philosophy and vain deceit."

Lest we be deceived like the razor clam, let us "be no more children, carried about with every wind of doctrine, by the sleight of men, and cunning craftiness, whereby they lie in wait to deceive." (Ephesians 4:14)

I ALWAYS LOOK FOR A NUMBER 12

I love watermelon. In the summer, I eat watermelon every night. However, there was one thing I did not understand about the watermelons I always bought. There is a number pasted on the pack of watermelon slices. Usually, it is ten or eleven or twelve. Until recently, I always wondered what was the meaning of the number.

Last Sunday, one of the church members explained it to me. The number shows the amount of sugar in the watermelon. In other words, the number reveals the level of sweetness of the watermelon. The higher the number, the sweeter the watermelon. The number of the sweetest watermelon is fifteen. The highest I have ever seen at my store is a twelve, so that is what I always look for when I buy watermelon.

What do you suppose would happen if God did the same thing? In other words, if God wrote the level of our righteousness on our forehead, what would be the level of our righteousness?

For example, in First Thessalonians 5:12-22 there is a list of fifteen commands that Christians should obey. There are commands such as "Be at peace among yourselves. Comfort the feebleminded. Support the weak. Be patient toward all men. See that none render evil for evil unto any man. Ever follow that which is good, both among yourselves, and to all men. Rejoice evermore. Pray without ceasing. In every thing give thanks. Prove all things. Hold fast that which is good. Abstain from all appearance of evil."

How many of these commands are we obeying? That number is the level of our righteousness.

I AM AN ALIEN!

There is something which I must confess to my family and friends. No one has known this until now, but I am an alien. Although I have only two eyes, my skin is not green, and there is no antenna sticking out of my head. I am an alien.

Wherever we go in Japan, foreigners have to carry a registration certificate with them. This certificate is written in Japanese and English. The first time I looked at my certificate, I was surprised. Usually, the Japanese word *gaikokujin* is translated "foreigner." However, my certificate does not say, "Foreigner Registration Certificate." It says, "Alien Registration Certificate." According to the government of Japan, I am an alien!

Actually, all people who believe in Christ are now aliens. In other words, we are no longer people of this world. Christ Himself said so three times in the Gospel of John.

"If ye were of the world, the world would love his own: but because ye are not of the world, but I have chosen you out of the world. (15:19) "I have given them thy word; and the world hath hated them, because they are not of the world, even as I am not of the world. They are not of the world, even as I am not of the world." (17:14 and 16)

The Bible says this about the saints listed in chapter 11 of Hebrews. "These all died in faith . . . and confessed that they were strangers and pilgrims on the earth." (11:13) Present-day Christians too need to be aware of the fact that we are "aliens" living in a world that is not our home. We are strangers and pilgrims on our way to God's country.

"I CAN SEE YOUR WINGS"

"Ken, please help me." It was the pitiful voice of a good friend. Her husband died five years ago, so she often calls me for assistance,

"What's the matter?" "I received a letter from the IRS in America and I do not understand the meaning. Please help me."

I drove to Yahata and read the letter. Just then, another American came, and together we explained the letter to her. He promised that he would prepare a reply to the IRS, so she was relieved.

Later, we went to lunch. While we were eating, I decided to tease her. "You were so worried that you could not sleep, but God sent two angels to help you." Laughing, she replied, "I can see your wings."

Of course, as soon as I mentioned angels, she mentioned wings. Most people believe that angels have wings. However, there is not one passage in the Bible that teaches that angels have wings. It was the artists of the Renaissance that gave wings to angels. Now the angels that appear in almost all picture books have wings.

According to Hebrews 1:14, angels are ministering spirits sent to serve people. I was able to serve my friend, so I referred to myself as an angel.

I do not know if angels really have wings or not, but Christians have wings. Those wings are the good things we do when we serve other people. Can the people around you see your wings? "Let your light so shine before men that they may see your good works (your wings), and glorify your Father which is in heaven." (Matthew 5:16)

KEN BOARD

I CAN'T FIND MY MONEY!

Last Sunday I preached at the Okinawa Bible Baptist Church. After the evening service, one of the men of the church handed me two envelopes with cash in them, one containing my love-offering and one with my travel expenses.

I thought I put the envelopes in my coat pocket, but when I looked for them in my coat pocket on Monday morning, they were not there. I checked each pocket two or three times but could not find the envelopes.

I looked in my briefcase and my suitcase but could not find the envelopes, so I was quite discouraged. Happily, I finally found them when I opened my Bible.

Just as I searched desperately for the envelopes, many people are searching desperately for that which has value. They search for something that will bring them peace and joy in pleasure, music education, sports, hobbies, riches and friends but are unable to find anything that has lasting value.

If you are one of those people, I urge you to look in the Bible. "The law of the Lord is perfect, converting the soul: the testimony of the Lord is sure, making wise the simple. The statutes of the Lord are right, rejoicing the heart: the commandment of the Lord is pure, enlightening the eyes. More to be desired are they than gold, yea, than much fine gold: sweeter also than honey and the honeycomb." (Psalm 19:7-8,10)

If you are having a hard time finding something that will bring you fulfillment, try opening the Bible.

"I DON'T HAVE TIME"

In the July 27th edition of the English newspaper there was an article that saddened me greatly. According to a survey conducted in Japan, the United States, China, and Korea, in 60% of the homes in Japan where there are elementary school children and middle school children, even when the family is together, they use cell phones and smart phones. This was the highest percentage among the four nations, twice as high as the United States.

44% of elementary school children and 37% of middle school children said that when they try to talk to their parents, the parents say, "I don't have time." How sad! The home where parents do not have time to talk with their children is a pitiful home. They give their children money and things, but they do not have time to talk with them! The most precious thing that parents can give to their children is time.

Let's make time to talk with our children. We may be tired after working all day, but let's make an effort to spend time with our children. Read books with them. Play games with them. Especially, listen to them.

100 years ago, parents spent 54% of their time with their children. Now it is 18%. According to statistics, the average father spends ten minutes a day with his children. Ten minutes! Of course, there is no passage in the Bible that says, "Spend time with your children," but Ephesians 6:4 instructs fathers to bring their children "up in the nurture and admonition of the Lord."

In order to follow these instructions, parents must spend time with their children and listen to them.

I FELL INTO HIS ARMS

The deliveryman brought a package to my home. After giving the package to me, he handed me the delivery receipt and asked me to sign it. Just as I reached for it, I lost my balance and fell backwards toward the door. If I had fallen all the way to the floor, I might have been seriously hurt, but the deliveryman put out his arms and caught me. I fell into his arms. The surprised deliveryman asked me over and over, "Are you all right?" I assured him that I was all right, but I was extremely embarrassed.

61 years ago, at a small Baptist church in Roanoke, Virginia, I fell into the arms of another person. When I received Christ as my Savior, my soul fell into His arms. Since that time, my soul has been protected in the strong arms of the Lord.

According to Psalm 89:13, the arm of the Lord is a mighty arm. Also, accorded to verse 24 of Jude, the Lord "is able to keep you from falling, and to present you faultless before the presence of his glory with exceeding joy."

There is a hymn entitled "Safe In The Arms Of Jesus."

Safe in the arms of Jesus,
Safe on His gentle breast;
There by His love o'ershaded,
Sweetly my soul shall rest.

When the child of God meets a severe trial and thinks he is about to fall, there is no need to fear. According to Deuteronomy 33:27, underneath us are the everlasting arms of the Lord.

I GOT MY GOLD BACK

I have been living in Japan for 47 years. For the first 35 years, the color of my driving license was blue. (A blue license indicates that the driver has had at least one violation during the past three years.) And then, I finally was able to get a gold license (a license for someone who had no violations during the past three years.) However, I caused two traffic accidents and I lost my gold license.

Last week I went to renew my license. When I looked at my new license, I shouted, "I did it! It's gold! I did it!" People waiting to receive their licenses laughed at me.

For the next three years I intend to be proud of my gold license. However, to tell the truth, I did not deserve a gold license. During the past three years, I drove over the speed limit many times. I ran red lights. I have a gold license only because there were no police cars around when I committed those violations.

It is the same with people who have been saved by faith in Christ. Not one of us deserved salvation. Every day we commit various sins. Although the police did not see my violations, God sees every one of our sins. In spite of that, the Lord gives salvation to all who believe in Christ. However, none of us can boast, "I did it! I'm saved! I did it!" In Ephesians 2:8-9 it is written, "For by grace are ye saved through faith; and that not of yourselves: it is the gift of God: Not of works, lest any man should boast."

If we have received forgiveness of sin and eternal life, let us boast not of our own goodness; rather, let us boast of God's amazing grace.

"I HAVE TO HELP HIM!"

Imagine this situation. You are sitting in the car with your father waiting for the train to pass. Just then, you see an old man fallen on the tracks. The train will come soon. What will you do?

A young lady placed in that situation said to her father, "I have to help him!" Her father replied, "Don't go. There is not enough time." However, she jumped out of the car and went to help the man. She was able to save him, but she was hit and killed by the train.

The young lady received a "Red Ribbon" medal from her country. This is a medal given to people who show extraordinary courage to save someone. Also, Japan awarded the "Silver Star" medal to her parents for their daughter's heroic action.

When I read this article about this young lady's sacrificial deed, I was reminded of the sacrifice that Christ paid for us. In Romans 5:8 it is written, "But God commendeth his love toward us, in that, while we were yet sinners, Christ died for us." If we are moved by the story of the sacrificial deed of this young lady, how much more should we be moved by the sacrificial deed of Christ! She gave her life to save one person. Christ gave His life to save all mankind!

Consider this too. She died to save the mortal body of one person, but Christ died to save the immortal soul of all who will believe in Him.

She received a medal from her country, a medal she justly deserved. What does the Savior who died for us deserve from us? Is it not our faith and obedience?

I HEARD ONLY ONE WORD

I had a question about my alien registration certificate, so I went to the Kokura Immigration Office. The man at the counter said, "Let me see your certificate." When he looked at it, he spoke words that stunned me. "Your period of residence ended on September first. You have been living in Japan illegally for two months."

The next words he spoke stunned me even more. "Bring your documents within a week. We will look over them and decide whether or not to deport you." The only word I heard was "deport." I thought, "Deport? Deport? No way. I cannot get deported with the Christmas services just a few weeks away."

I frantically gathered all my documents and went back to the office two days later. I was told to sit down and wait while they decided if they would accept my documents or not. I waited only 15 minutes, but it was a long, long 15 minutes. They accepted my documents and approved a 3-year extension of my stay in Japan.

There are occasions when people are deported from a country or evicted from a house. However, the person who believes in Christ is going to a country where no one will ever be deported. According to John 14:2, Christ is preparing a home for us in the city built by God. (Hebrews 11:10) It is our eternal home in heaven. (Second Corinthians 5:1)

Going to the country of God where no one will be deported or evicted from his home is the hope of every Christian. It will be exactly as it is written in the last part of the famous 23rd Psalm. "We shall dwell in the house of the Lord forever."

"I LOVE YOU!"

When I left the airport in Taiwan and headed to the airport for my flight back to Japan, I went by taxi to the airport. The taxi driver was very thoughtful. First, he asked me in English, "Time?" In other words, "Is the time okay. Are you in a hurry?" I replied, "Time OK."

Next, he asked me, "Air OK?" In other words, "Is the temperature in the cab OK?" I replied, "Air OK."

When we arrived at the airport, he unloaded my luggage for me. Although tipping is not a custom in Taiwan, I gave him a tip. I do not know how much I gave him, but it must have been a very nice tip. With a big smile on his face, he said, "I love you!"

What do you think? Did that driver really love me? Of course not. He said, "I love you!" because I gave him a tip.

Before we criticize him let's ask ourselves this question. Why do I love God? Perhaps we say, "I love you," to God because He blesses us, or maybe we say, "I love you," to God because He answers our prayers. This kind of love is not true love.

The Christian who truly loves God is not the Christian who loves God because of what God does for him but the Christian who loves God because of who He is. In Exodus 34:6 the Bible teaches us that God is merciful and gracious, abundant in goodness and truth. "Gracious is the Lord, and righteous; yea, our God is merciful." (Psalm 116:5) The Christian who understands that the God in whom we believe is this kind of God is the Christian who can say to God from his heart, "I love you."

I MET "CALEB"

———— ❧ ————

I am seventy-six years old and am suffering from various illnesses. The neuropathy in my feet has especially become a major problem. In addition, I tire quite easily, so now and then I am tempted to retire.

However, recently I was greatly encouraged by someone ten years older than I am. His name is George King. He is an eighty-six-year-old missionary who has been doing evangelism in Japan since 1960. He too is suffering from various illnesses. When he walks, he has to use a cane, and there is a large cast on his left arm, so doing such simple things as buttoning a shirt is difficult for him.

The other day I had the privilege of having fellowship with him. During our several hours together, there was no talk of retirement. Surprisingly, he spent most of the time talking about his plans for future evangelism.

As I listened to him, I remembered the words of an eighty-five-year-old man named Caleb written in chapter 14 of Joshua. "Now therefore give me this mountain, whereof the Lord spake in that day; for thou heardest in that day how the Anakims were there, and that the cities were great and fenced: if so be the Lord will be with me, then I shall be able to drive them out, as the Lord said." (verse 12)

Please remember that there is no age limit in our service to the Lord. We must not think that only young people can serve the Lord. In spite of our age, let's serve the Lord faithfully until His coming. We must not become "rocking chair Christians" who are waiting on the Lord to come. Like Caleb, let's find a mountain that we too can climb and become "mountain-climbing Christians."

I NEEDED ANOTHER EYE

I cannot prove this, but I think the apostle Paul distributed tracts and flyers in the South Kokura section of Kitakyushu City at least once, for in Philippians 3:2 he wrote, "Beware of dogs."

Of course, I am joking, but lately I have been passing out flyers in the Yoshida section of South Kokura. Many people in Yoshida have dogs, so every time I distribute flyers there, I am frightened by a dog.

The other day, as I neared the mailbox at a certain house, suddenly a dog rushed all the way to the gate and began barking at me. The mailbox was right by the gate, so I had one eye on the dog and the other eye on the mailbox. Unfortunately, there was no eye to look at the stairs, so I stumbled and rolled down the stairs and out into the street. I needed another eye.

As we are walking the path of life, there are times when we need another eye. Storms crash against us from all directions and we are in danger of stumbling. Thankfully, the Bible teaches us that we do have another eye. Our other eye is the God in whom we believe. In Second Chronicles 16:9 it is written, "For the eyes of the Lord run to and fro throughout the whole earth, to shew himself strong in the behalf of them whose heart is perfect toward him."

In First Peter 3:12 it is written, "For the eyes of the Lord are over the righteous, and his ears are open unto their prayers." The eyes of the Lord are over the person who has been made righteous by faith in Christ. When we are assailed by difficult circumstances and do not know which way to turn, the eyes of the Lord will lead us to the right path.

I SAT WHERE HE SAT

"Then I came to them of the captivity at Telabib, that dwelt by the river of Chebar, and **I sat where they sat,** and remained there astonished among them seven days." (Ezekiel 3:15)

When I attended the memorial service for Missionary Bill Neel, I remembered this passage. After the service, Pastor Enomoto took me to Brother Neel's church. Two church members were there, so we were able to go inside. One of the members pointed to a chair and said, "The last year of his life Pastor Neel was unable to stand and preach, so he sat in this chair and taught us the Bible."

I asked the church members, "May I sit in his chair?" They gave me permission, so I sat in his chair for a while and tried to imagine the last year of his life. He was 86 years old. He came to Japan in 1964 and served the Lord faithfully for 53 years. Even if he had left Japan when his health began to fail, no one could have blamed him, but he continued to preach the gospel in Japan until he went home to be with the Lord. Why?

In Romans 10:1 Paul wrote, "Brethren, my heart's desire and prayer to God for Israel is, that they might be saved." To the apostle Paul, "they" were the Jews. To Missionary Bill Neel, "they" were the Japanese. Because he loved the Japanese and desired their salvation, he preached the gospel to the very end.

Who is "they" to you? Your parents? Your children? Your brothers and sisters? Your friends? Whoever "they" is to us, let's make their salvation the desire of our heart and pray fervently to God for their salvation.

I SAT WITH THE "ENEMY"

Last week I went to Yahoo Dome with a missionary named Tamura to see the baseball game between the Hawks and the Tigers. I am a fanatical Hawks fan and he is a fanatical Tigers fan. He asked me, "Is it okay if we sit in the section where fans of the Tigers sit?" I wanted to sit with the fans of the Hawks, but since he was paying for the tickets, I agreed to sit with the "enemy."

Even though I sat in the Tigers' fan section, I wore my Hawks' baseball cap and rooted enthusiastically for the Hawks. Each time the Hawks scored a run, I jumped to my feet and shouted with joy. In the middle of the seventh inning, I stood and sang the Hawks' team song with the other Hawks' fans. (The Hawks won 4-0.)

One night, Peter, a disciple of Christ, sat with the enemy. "Then took they him, and led him, and brought him into the high priest's house. And Peter followed afar off. And when they had kindled a fire in the midst of the hall, and were set down together, Peter sat down among them." (Luke 22:54-55) As he was sitting with the enemies of Christ, three times he had the opportunity to stand up and declare his allegiance to Christ, but all three times he denied his relationship with Christ. (Luke 22:56-50)

How about us? We cheer for Christ at church, but do we cheer for Him when we are sitting with the enemy? In other words, do we testify of our faith in Christ when we are with those who are not Christians? In Psalm 109:30 David said, "I will greatly praise the Lord with my mouth; yea, I will praise him among the multitude." When we too are among the multitude, even if they are the "enemy," let's stand up and cheer for Christ.

"I WILL BRING THE OTTERS"

Curry rice is not part of the diet of most Americans. Some people may go to an Indian restaurant to eat curry rice, but very few people fix curry rice and eat it at home. This is especially true of people in the South where I live. I ate curry rice for the first time after I came to Japan. Now I occasionally go to a curry restaurant when I go out to eat. When I do eat it, there is one thing I always like to eat with it. It is a scallion (called *rakkyoo* in Japanese). If I eat scallions with my curry rice, it is twice as delicious.

One Sunday when we were talking about the meal for the next Sunday, we decided to make curry rice. I said, "I will bring the *rakko*." The church members burst out laughing. When they were finally able to stop laughing, they explained, "Pastor, we eat *rakkyoo* (scallions) with curry rice. A *rakko* is an animal that lives in the sea." Because I left out the Y in *rakkyoo*, I had said, "I will bring the otters."

As I thought about my humorous mistake, I sensed a new appreciation of the Bible. If the writers of the Bible had added or left out even one letter, the meaning might have been as different as the difference between scallions and otters. This is why the words in Matthew 5:18 affirm the accuracy of the Bible. "For verily I say unto you, Till heaven and earth pass, one jot or one tittle shall in no wise pass from the law, till all be fulfilled."

Because we know that not one jot or tittle will pass from the Word of God, we can trust in the Bible at all times in all circumstances. "It is easier for heaven and earth to pass, than one tittle of the law to fail." (Luke 16:17)

IN THE CLOUDS

Unfortunately, the typhoon and I happened to go to Tokyo the same day. The weather was clear until we approached Tokyo, but suddenly the plane was surrounded by clouds and began to shake. Many of the passengers were becoming anxious. I was one of them. Just then we heard the voice of the pilot. "From here there will be a lot of turbulence, but this plane is safe. Please be at ease." During the next several minutes, he repeated this message several times. "This plane is safe. Please be at ease."

Praying for a safe landing, I kept my eyes on the monitor, but I could see nothing but clouds. Suddenly the clouds disappeared and the airport appeared on the monitor. When the plane landed safely, many of the passengers applauded.

From time to time, the Christian life is similar to an airplane flying in the clouds. We are surrounded by difficulties and trials. Day after day our hearts are filled with anxiety and fear. Just when we think we cannot endure any longer, we hear the voice of our Pilot. "These things I have spoken unto you, that in me ye might have peace. In the world ye shall have tribulation: but be of good cheer; I have overcome the world." (John 16:33)

When we are surrounded by the clouds of tribulation and wondering how long the cloudy days will continue, if we will listen quietly, the words of our Pilot will remove the anxiety from our heart and give us peace. "Peace I leave with you, my peace I give unto you: not as the world giveth, give I unto you. Let not your heart be troubled, neither let it be afraid." (John 14:27)

INCIDENT ON TOP OF A VOLCANO

Whenever an American comes to Kyushu to visit me, I usually take him to one of four places: Sarakura Mountain in Kitakyushu City, Nagasaki, the area called "Hell" in Beppu, or the volcano at Mount Aso. When I took one pastor to see the volcano, there was a life-threatening incident.

We were standing on top of Mount Aso looking down into the core of the crater. Suddenly, the direction of the wind changed and we were enveloped in a cloud of sulfur smoke. Struggling to breathe, the pastor shouted, "I have asthma. Get me out of here as quickly as you can!"

We hurried to the car. He was still struggling to breathe, so as I drove as fast as I could, we opened all the windows to let in as much air as possible. After a while, his breathing became normal. He told me, "I have an inhaler, but I left it in my hotel room."

There are times when our souls face a similar danger. We are enveloped in a cloud of trials and begin to choke spiritually. When we face this experience, we must not forget that there is only one thing that can help us. In Psalm 119:93 David wrote, "I will never forget thy precepts: for with them thou hast quickened me."

Knowing his weakness, the pastor forgot his inhaler. Likewise, knowing our weaknesses, we must not forget to read God's Word regularly. "My soul fainteth for thy salvation: but I hope in thy word. Mine eyes fail for thy word, saying, When wilt thou comfort me? For I am become like a bottle in the smoke; yet do I not forget thy statutes." (Psalm 119:81-83). Only the Word of God can give us the spiritual "air" we need to survive in the "smoke" of the many trials of life.

IT WAS DELIGHTFUL . . . BUT

Whenever I think about the Kokua church, these words in Psalm 133:1 come to my mind. "Behold, how good and how pleasant it is for brethren to dwell together in unity!" Singing and studying the Bible together is delightful. Eating lunch together is delightful. The fellowship after lunch is delightful. Participating in various ministries in the afternoon is delightful.

It is delightful . . . BUT we must not forget the most important purpose of this church. It is written in Mark 16:15. "Go ye into all the world and preach the gospel to every creature."

Recently a friend and I went to an all-you-can-eat restaurant. The meal was delicious, and the fellowship was delightful. Later my friend drove me home. I got out of his car and, searching for my keys, walked toward my home. Just then I realized something awful. My overcoat with my keys in the pocket was still at the restaurant!

I shouted, "Wait!" to my friend as he pulled away. Thankfully, he heard my shout. He drove me back to the restaurant, so I was able to get my overcoat that had my house key, my car key, and the church key in the pocket.

I had become engrossed in the delightful meal and forgotten something important. Our church must not make the same mistake. Let's enjoy our worship and fellowship at church, but we must not forget the important mission that we received from the Lord. "Go out into the highways and hedges, and compel them to come in, that my house may be filled." (Luke 14:23)

IT WAS JUST ONE MIKAN BUT . . .

We have lunch together every Sunday at the Kokura church. Some people bring homemade lunches and others, like me, bring lunches they bought at a convenient store.

Brother and Sister Yamaguchi sat beside me and ate lunches she had made at home. After they finished eating, he brought out two mikans (a mikan is a citrus fruit similar to a tangerine) and said, "How about a mikan?" and gave one of them to me. Since then, he has done that several times.

It was just one mikan, but to me, it was a sign of love, so the mikan was very delicious.

Another man who comes to the Friday night English class handed me a bag and said, "This is from my wife." There was a soda and some cookies in the bag. Those items probably would not have cost five dollars at the store, but to me, they were symbols of love, so they were quite valuable to me.

When we went on a picnic recently, one family fixed the lunch for me and a friend from America. The lunch with their love mixed into it was delicious.

In Matthew 10:42 Christ said, "Whosoever shall give to drink unto one of these little ones a cup of cold water only in the name of a disciple, verily I say unto you, he shall in no wise lose his reward." Whether it is one drink of water or one mikan, the small things we do to show love to others can encourage them greatly.

IT WAS TRUE

These words were written on the billboard of a restaurant across the street from the Nakagawa church: "Delicious. Cheap. Filling. Satisfying." Every time I saw that sign, I would wonder, "Is it true?"

Last month, when I attended a special meeting at the church, several of us went to that restaurant. It was exactly as the sign said. The sweet and sour pork dish that I ordered was delicious. The price was cheap. It was quite filling. It was very satisfying. Everyone who ate there gave it high marks.

The restaurant that puts out a sign that says "Delicious, Cheap, Filling. Satisfying." has the responsibility to provide meals that are delicious, cheap, filling and satisfying. Likewise, the person who puts out the billboard "I am a Christian" has the responsibility to live a life that is true to that billboard. He must manifest deeds that prove his words. In the Bible it is written, "If we say that we have fellowship with him, and walk in darkness, we lie, and do not the truth:" (First John 1:6)

There were four words written on the restaurant billboard, but there are nine words written on the billboard of the Christian: Love. Joy. Peace. Longsuffering. Gentleness. Goodness. Faith. Meekness. Temperance. (Galatians 5:22-23) People who compare our conduct and attitude to this billboard should be able to give us high marks.

"He that saith he abideth in him ought himself also so to walk, even as he walked." (First John 2:6) We have a responsibility to manifest a lifestyle that is consistent with our profession of faith so that people will compare our conduct with our billboard and say, "It is true."

IT WOULD NOT COME ON
WHEN IT WAS COLD

———— ❧ ————

I attend the ladies meeting at the Kitakyushu church on the second and fourth Saturdays each month. After Pastor Miyake teaches the Bible lesson, I teach English. One day, when I entered the room, it was dark, so I turned on the light. There are two lights in the room, but only one of them came on. When the ladies meeting began, the light was still not on. About fifty minutes into the meeting, it finally lit up.

I asked Pastor Miyake, "What's wrong with that light?" He replied, "When the weather is warm, it will come on right away, but when the weather is cold, it will not come on."

The Christian should be careful that his faith does not resemble that light. In Matthew 5:16 Jesus said, "Let your light so shine before men, that they may see your good works, and glorify your Father which is in heaven."

Because Christ has given us this important mission, let's let our light shine when it is warm and also when it is cold. In other words, in "warm" times when we are in the midst of blessings and in "cold" times when we are in the midst of trials, let's maintain a faith that is shining brightly.

In Philippians 2:15 it is written, "That ye may be blameless and harmless, the sons of God, without rebuke, in the midst of a crooked and perverse nation, among whom ye shine as lights in the world."

There are times when our life may resemble an extremely cold winter day. Even then, let's continue to shine. Be faithful "in season" and "out of season." (Second Timothy 4:2)

IT'S A WONDERFUL LIFE

If you had to choose the title of one movie to summarize your life so far, which movie title would you choose?

I would choose "It's a Wonderful Life." Of course, I have had some grave experiences: the divorce of my parents, the sudden death of my father, my mother, and my wife, and my battle with cancer and other illnesses. However, because I believed in Christ when I was 13, and because I dedicated my life to the Lord when I was 17, my life became a wonderful life.

Because I obeyed the voice of the Lord, I was able to visit many churches and form friendships that have lasted more than fifty years with many pastors and missionaries.

Because I obeyed the voice of the Lord, I was able to experience a new culture and work for the Lord together with many wonderful Japanese Christians.

Because I obeyed the voice of the Lord, I have seen spectacular scenery that most Americans have never seen. I have walked on Mount Fuji. I have seen the Sky Tree in Tokyo and the magnificent buildings in Kyoto. I have stood on the top of Mount Aso and looked down into the core of the largest volcanic crater in the world.

The secret of a wonderful life is to obey the voice of the Lord and walk with Him. "Obey my voice, and I will be your God, and ye shall be my people: and walk ye in all the ways that I have commanded you, that it may be well unto you." (Jeremiah 7:23)

JESUS AND MARY . . . AND BUDDHA?

———— ❧ ————

During December, the church displays a Christmas scene that features dolls of Joseph, Mary, and baby Jesus. This year we decided to do a "living" display. On Christmas Eve, two of the church members took the place of the Joseph and Mary dolls.

Several weeks before Christmas, the ladies made costumes for Joseph and Mary. When they tried on the costumes, the ladies looked at the lady wearing Mary's blue robe and remarked how beautiful she was. However, when they looked at the man wearing Joseph's yellow robe, they roared with laughter. He looked exactly like the Buddha that we often see in pictures! I yelled, "What! Jesus and Mary and Buddha in the manger? This won't work!" The ladies changed the color of his robe so he would not look like Buddha.

Buddha, Mohammed, and Confucius may have been splendid people, but there is no one who can compare with Christ.

First of all, Christ alone never sinned. "Who did no sin, neither was guile found in his mouth." (First Peter 2:22)

Also, Christ alone solved the problem of sin. When Christ died on the cross for our sins, He solved the problem of sin. "But God commendeth his love toward us, in that, while we were yet sinners, Christ died for us." (Romans 5:8)

Therefore, the Bible declares, "Neither is there salvation in any other: for there is none other name under heaven given among men, whereby we must be saved." (Acts 4:12)

JUST THREE MORE FEET

It was the bottom of the eighth inning of the playoff game between the Fukuoka Softbank Hawks, the team I root for, and the Seibu Lions. The Hawks were leading 3-1, so I was happy. The Lions had runners on first and third with two outs. When I saw the next batter, my joy turned into fear. Nakamura, the Lions' cleanup hitter who had already hit a home run earlier in the game, was coming to bat. If he hit another home run, the Hawks would be losing 4-3 with only one inning left.

Just as I feared, Nakamura's bat hit the ball cleanly. It soared toward center field. I yelled, "Oh no!" and held my breath. The Hawks' center field raced back and, with his back against the wall, caught the ball. If the ball had gone three feet further, it would have been a home run, but it came up short.

"It came up short" – these are words that describe the spiritual condition of everyone. "For all have sinned and come short of the glory of God." (Romans 3:23) Even if we live as morally right a life as possible in order to go to heaven, we will come up short, for we all are sinners by nature. Even if we do as many good works as possible, we will still come up short. "For by grace are ye saved through faith; and that not of yourselves: it is the gift of God: Not of works, lest any man should boast." (Ephesians 2:8-9)

There is only one way to enter heaven. That one way is faith in Jesus Christ who died on the cross for our sins. The person who trusts in his own righteousness as a method of entering heaven will end up the same as the ball Nakamaura hit. He may get within three feet of heaven, but he will come up just a little short.

LANDSLIDE!

Lately heavy rain in Kyushu has caused several landslides destroying property and taking lives. When I saw a picture of one of the landslides in the newspaper, I remembered my experience with a landslide. One of the men of the church had gone to the island of Shikoku with me to search for a good location for Summer Camp.

We drove way up into the mountains. On the way down the mountain we saw a vending machine and decided to stop and get something to drink. As we stood there enjoying our drinks, we heard a rumbling sound down the mountain and wondered what it was.

We got back in the car and continued down the mountain. As we went around a sharp curve, we slammed on the brakes and looked ahead in amazement. There was some dirt and a large rock, larger than my car, in the middle of the road. We looked at one another and realized that if we had not stopped at that vending machine, we might have been at that very spot when the landslide occurred. We bowed our heads and thanked the Lord for His protection.

God often protects us through unexpected methods that we do not even realize. For example, we are irritated because we did not make the green light, but that red light may have been God's method of protecting us from an accident.

We will probably be amazed when we get to heaven and see the many times God protected us from harm. "The angel of the Lord encampeth round about them that fear him, and delivereth them." (Psalm 34:7) Let us be aware of and thankful for the Lord's daily protection.

KEN BOARD

LEFT BEHIND

Just before the last service of Summer Camp began, one pastor rushed up to the songleader and said, "The children aren't here!" The service was supposed to begin with a special song by the children.

I said to several pastors sitting behind me, "Do you suppose the rapture took place?" One pastor replied, "Then that means we were left behind." We all laughed. Just then, the children came on stage, so we were relieved.

A popular series of books describes the experiences of people who are left behind when the rapture takes place. Much of the content of the books is fiction, but the fact that some people will be left behind at the rapture is not fiction. It is a true fact written in the Bible. "Then shall two be in the field; the one shall be taken, and the other left. Two women shall be grinding at the mill; the one shall be taken, and the other left. Watch therefore: for ye know not what hour your Lord doth come." (Matthew 24:40-42)

In this passage, the person who is "taken" is the person who admits his sins and believes in Jesus Christ who died on the cross for our sins. The person who is "left" is the person who, at the time of the second coming of Christ, has not yet believed in Christ.

When one of the pastors jokingly said, "Then that means we were left behind," we all laughed. However, to the person who is actually left behind when Jesus comes again, it is no laughing matter. "Therefore be ye also ready: for in such an hour as ye think not the Son of man cometh." (Matthew 24:44)

LEFT OR RIGHT?

As we neared the town of Kurume, I said to the guy sitting beside me, "There is a large idol in this town." A few minutes later we saw the idol towering over the town. I told him, "A little bit further ahead, we can see the idol clearly on the right side of the road."

A girl sitting in the back seat spoke up and said, "It's on the left side." I replied, "No, it's on the right side." She replied, "I think it is on the left."

Certainly, as you approach Kurume, the statue appears to be on the left side, so she thought it was on the left. but I drive that road every time I go to Kagoshima to visit my son, so I knew it was on the right. Her opinion was based on what she thought. My opinion was based on what I knew.

In Second Corinthians 5:7 it is written, "For we walk by faith, not by sight:" The faith of the Christian is based not upon what he thinks but upon what he knows. "We know that all things work together for good to them that love God, to them who are the called according to his purpose." (Romans 8;28)

"Therefore, my beloved brethren, be ye stedfast, unmoveable, always abounding in the work of the Lord, forasmuch as ye know that your labour is not in vain in the Lord." (First Corinthians 15:58)

"For we know that if our earthly house of this tabernacle were dissolved, we have a building of God, an house not made with hands, eternal in the heavens." (Second Corinthians 5:1)

Is your faith an "I think" faith or an "I know" faith based on the Bible?

LOST IN THE MOUNTAINS

I left for Summer Camp at nine o'clock with one of the ladies and her teenage son. We planned to go through Hiyamizu Pass, but the road was closed because of damage from heavy rains.

We had no choice but to go through Hiyamizu Tunnel to route 386 and then head toward Amagi. On the way, there was a sign for Yasu Koogen, so we turned left but soon found ourselves lost. We asked directions from a lady walking on the road, but when we went in that direction, we came to another road that was closed.

Next, we asked directions from a man who was familiar with the roads in that area, but when we went the way that he told us to go, we came to another place where the road was closed. Then the teenage son took the GPS in his hand and found us a road that went to the Camp. We finally arrived about noon. A trip that should have taken ninety minutes took three hours. If it had not been for the GPS, we might still be wandering around in those mountains.

There are times in life too when the road we are walking comes to a dead end. We are like a traveler lost in a mountain forest. Our heart is lost in a forest of fear and confusion. What we need is a GPS for our heart. At that time, the Word of God that we have stored in our heart becomes our GPS. "Thy word is a lamp unto my feet, and a light unto my path." (Psalm 119:105)

When we come to a dead end in life, instead of becoming flustered and making a hasty decision, let's pray the prayer in Psalm 119:133. "Order my steps in thy word:"

ME? AN OLD PERSON? THERE MUST BE SOME MISTAKE

—————— ❧ ——————

I received a post card that I did not like in the mail. It said, "Elderly Person Driving Test Notice." I thought, "Elderly person? There must be some mistake. There is no elderly person living in this house." However, the post card had my name on it.

I was shocked. It was the first time I had been addressed as an "elderly person." I do not want to admit that I am getting old., but it is a fact. I am an elderly person. Next year I will be seventy years old. According to the post card, all people over seventy years of age must go to driving school to renew their driver's license.

Because I have a "young" personality, I have never considered myself to be an elderly person. My body is sixty-nine years old, but my heart is twenty-nine. Sadly, my sixty-nine-year-old body will no longer listen to my twenty-nine-year-old heart. When my heart tells my body to do something, my body answers, "You're kidding, right?"

Although I am getting old, I want to continue to serve the Lord faithfully. There is no retirement age for Christians. As long as we are able, let's do some sort of service for the Lord at our church.

In his letter to Titus, Paul wrote a special exhortation for elderly people. "That the aged men be sober, grave, temperate, sound in faith, in charity, in patience. The aged women likewise, that they be in behaviour as becometh holiness, not false accusers, not given to much wine, teachers of good things." (2:2-3)

Elderly? Yes. "Washed up." No.

MISSING

According to police reports, 2565 mountain climbers went missing last year. Of those who went missing, 249 people died. 35 people are still missing. 927 people were injured. 1254 people were found safe. They went missing for various reasons. 42% of them got lost. 15% fell from a high place. 14% tripped and fell. 8% got sick. 5% became exhausted.

The reasons the mountain climbers went missing are similar to the reasons why some Christians are now missing from church. Some lose their way and go missing because they do not read the Bible which is a lamp unto our feet and a lamp unto our path. Psalm 119:105)

Some Christians are missing because they became proud and fell. "Pride goeth before destruction, and an haughty spirit before a fall." (Proverbs 16:18)

Because the Word of God is not in their hearts, some Christians stumble and go missing. According to Psalm 37:31, it is the Word of God that keeps our feet from sliding.

There are Christians who become spiritually sick and go missing. Psalm 41:4 teaches us that sin is the cause of their spiritual sickness.

Finally, some Christians go missing because they do not wait on the Lord and lose the strength to continue. "They that wait upon the Lord shall renew their strength; they shall mount up with wings as eagles; they shall run, and not be weary; and they shall walk, and not faint." (Isaiah 40:31)

Let's be careful lest we become one of the "missing" Christians.

MORE THAN ENOUGH

At the Kokura church, we have lunch together every Sunday. When the Wyatt family was still in Japan, Cristy fixed my lunch every week. After they returned to America for furlough, I intended to buy my lunch at a convenience store. However, now one of the ladies makes my lunch.

The meal she prepares for me is delicious. Many times, it is more than enough, so I cannot eat it all. I take the leftovers home, so the meal that she provides for me becomes my lunch and my dinner.

When I eat her meals that are more than enough, I remember two Bible passages. First, I remember Ephesians 3:20-21. "Now unto him that is able to do exceeding <u>abundantly above all that we ask or think</u>, according to the power that worketh in us, Unto him be glory in the church by Christ Jesus throughout all ages, world without end."

The other passage is Second Corinthians 9:8 "God is able to make all grace abound toward you; that ye, always having all sufficiency in all things, may abound to every good work:"

There is no need for the Christian to live a life of want. In Psalm 23:1 David wrote, "The Lord is my shepherd; I shall not want." If our way of living pleases the Lord, He will give us His love, grace, and mercy in abundance. It is not the will of the Lord for the Christian to be a spiritual beggar.

In John 10:10 Christ said this about His sheep. "I am come that they might have life, and that they might have it more abundantly." Abundant life – a life where the blessings of God are more than enough.

MURDER BY BAPTISM

Among the things that a missionary must do, there is one thing that I just cannot seem to do skillfully – baptizing people who have believed in Christ. I do not know why, but I am unable to do it smoothly. It was the same way this last baptism. As I was baptizing a man, my hand slipped from his face to his throat.

Later, when we looked at the pictures of the baptism, everyone laughed. His eyes were closed and my hand was around his throat. It looked like I was trying to choke him to death. I gave the title "Murder by Baptism" to the picture and jokingly told him, "I was just trying to send you to heaven right away."

Consider my joke seriously. What if we could go to heaven as soon as we were baptized? Think about it. The minute we came up out of the water, we would be in heaven. We could avoid all of the trials and troubles of the Christian life.

Of course, this is not the plan of God. His plan is explained in Romans 6:4. "Therefore we are buried with him by baptism into death: that like as Christ was raised up from the dead by the glory of the Father, even so <u>we also should walk in newness of life</u>."

If we went to heaven as soon as we were baptized, there would be no one left to preach the gospel to people who have yet to believe in Christ, so God leaves us here to walk in newness of life and become His witnesses. When people become aware of our new way of living, our new way of talking, and our new way of thinking, we shall be able to introduce them to the God who made us new creatures through faith in Christ.

MY CANE CAME IN HANDY

When I went to Taiwan last month, I was looking forward to meeting my good friend, Brother Sakai. However, on the way to meet him, there were some things to which I was not looking forward. One was going through passport control because there is always a long line there. When I have to wait a long time in a long line, because of the neuropathy, my feet hurt very much.

That day, I took my cane with me. When the person at passport control saw my cane, he said to me, "Come with me," He led me to the very front of the line. From now on, whenever I go to a place where there is the possibility of waiting a long time in a long line, I shall take my cane with me.

In the Bible we can see two instances when a cane came in handy. The first instance is recorded in chapter four of Exodus when God manifested His power to Moses by changing his staff (like a cane) into a snake and then changing it back again.

The second time a cane came in handy is recorded in chapter fourteen of Exodus. "Lift thou up thy rod, and stretch out thine hand over the sea, and divide it: and the children of Israel shall go on dry ground through the midst of the sea."

God has a cane too. David wrote these words about the cane of God: "Thy rod and thy staff they comfort me." (Psalm 23:4) The rod and staff are symbols of the power of God. Because we know that we are protected by the power of God (First Peter 1:5), we are comforted even in the midst of a grievous trial.

MY NEIGHBOR'S DOG HATES ME

I moved into this house eight years ago, From the first day, the neighbor's dog barked at me every time he saw me. I thought the dog would eventually get used to me and stop barking, but eight years later he still barks at me. I have tried many times to be his friend, but when I go near to him, he growls at me. When friends come to visit me, he allows them to get close to him and pet him, but he will not allow me to do it.

I finally figured out that the dog barked at me because he wanted me to notice him, so I decided to try talking to the dog. When I leave the house, if I say, "How are you today? What's the matter?" the dog will stop barking and look at me. He just wants me to pay attention to him.

Don't you think there are a lot of people in the world who resemble my neighbor's dog? All alone, they spend each day wishing for someone, even just one person, to pay attention to them. In their heart they are crying out, "Please see me! Please acknowledge my existence!"

In verse 4 of Psalm 142 the words of David express their loneliness. "I looked on my right hand, and beheld, but there was no man that would know me: refuge failed me; no man cared for my soul." When we, like David, begin to think, "There is no one who cares about me," let us remember the promise of God written in Hebrews 13:5. "I will never leave thee, nor forsake thee."

When no one else will see us and pay attention to us, the Lord will pay attention to us and see us. "Behold, the eye of the Lord is upon them that fear him, upon them that hope in his mercy;" (Psalm 33:18)

MY NEW FEET

For several years now I have suffered from neuropathy, a disease of the nervous system. The main symptoms are numbness and pain in my feet. I am especially perturbed over the influence of this problem on my evangelism. Before I contracted neuropathy, I could distribute hundreds of flyers and tracts in one day. Now, my feet begin to ache after I have distributed about a hundred flyers.

However, this year the Lord gave me some new feet. Since May, Missionaries Mike and Cristy Wyatt have been working with me at the Kokura church. Mike is young and full of energy, so he distributes a lot of flyers every day.

The other day when we went to distribute flyers together, Mike distributed 150 flyers. I intended to distribute 100, but after 79 flyers my feet were hurting so much that I had to stop. Mike became my feet and distributed the remaining 21 flyers for me.

Just as Mike has become my new feet, each Christian has the responsibility to become the feet of God. Before returning to heaven, Christ gave us the command to "go into all the world and preach the gospel to every creature." (Mark 16:15) He is no longer on the earth, so you and I must become the feet of Christ and go into all the world.

There is a poem entitled *God Has No Hands*:

God has no hands but our hands to do His work today
God has no feet but our feet to leads others in His way
God has no voice but our voice to tell others how He died
And, God has no help but our help to lead them to His side.

MY NUMBER

Lately, when I read the newspaper, I don't know if I am reading the newspaper or the Bible. For example, look at these passages in chapter 24 of Matthew:

"For many shall come in my name, saying, I am Christ; and shall deceive many." (verse 5) "And ye shall hear of wars and rumours of wars: see that ye be not troubled: for all these things must come to pass, but the end is not yet. For nation shall rise against nation, and kingdom against kingdom: and there shall be famines, and pestilences, and earthquakes, in divers places." (verses 6-7)

Articles similar to these passages appear in the newspaper almost daily. In the March 3rd newspaper, there was an article that amazes anyone who knows the Bible well. It seems that the Japanese government has passed a bill that will give each citizen an identification number. It will be called "MY NUMBER."

The instant I read this, I shouted, "It's Revelation!" The prophecies of Revelation are beginning to be fulfilled. "And he causeth all, both small and great, rich and poor, free and bond, to receive a <u>mark</u> in their right hand, or in their foreheads: And that no man might buy or sell, save he that had the mark, or the name of the beast, or the number of his name." (Revelation 13:16-17)

Because we know that the second coming of Christ is near, let's heed the admonition in First John 2:28. "LIttle children, abide in him; that, when he shall appear, we may have confidence, and not be ashamed before him at his coming."

MY RAVEN

"Get thee hence, and turn thee eastward, and hide thyself by the brook Cherith, that is before Jordan. And it shall be, that thou shalt drink of the brook; and I have commanded the ravens to feed thee there. So he went and did according unto the word of the Lord: for he went and dwelt by the brook Cherith, that is before Jordan. And the ravens brought him bread and flesh in the morning, and bread and flesh in the evening; and he drank of the brook." (First Kings 17:2-6)

There is a "raven" who brings me food too. From last year, Pastor Inaba's wife, Satomi, has been bringing me a meal every Thursday. Since my wife went home to be with the Lord, my biggest problem has been meals. Mrs. Inaba knows this, so she brings me a basket of food. There is usually enough for two or three days. Usually, I eat only meals I can cook in the microwave, so her home-cooked meals are very delicious.

I have some other "ravens" too. There is usually some delicious bread or cake from Mrs. Shiokawa in the basket that Mrs. Inaba brings me. In addition, when I go to the ladies meeting at Kitakyushu Bible Baptist Church on the second and fourth Saturdays of the month, Pastor Miyake's wife, Yooko, fixes me a delicious lunch. Last Monday, Brother Atonakasuji's wife fixed me a delicious meal.

When we, like Elijah, obey the Lord, our needs will be supplied. In Psalm 34:9-10 David wrote, "O fear the Lord, ye his saints: for there is no want to them that fear him. The young lions do lack, and suffer hunger: but they that seek the Lord shall not want any good thing." Has the Lord told you something to do? If you will obey Him, the Lord is already preparing a "raven" to bring you a blessing.

NEED TO THROW OUT SOME TRASH?

In America people do not separate their garbage. They put all garbage (food, plastic, bottles, and cans) into the same trash bag. Also, they do not have to buy special bags (in Japan we are required to buy special trash bags).

Also, in Japan we are required to divide the garbage, so there are four garbage bags in my kitchen – one for food, one for plastic, one for plastic bottles, and one for cans and glass bottles.

In the kitchen of the Grace Baptist Church in Nagashima there is only one trash bag. Except for leftover food, all trash is put into that one bag. The first time I saw the church people dispose of leftover food, I was surprised. They just open the kitchen window and throw the food outside. The church is surrounded by woods and fields, so the animals and birds that live there come and eat the food.

Perhaps it would be good if we opened our heart now and then and threw away the "trash" in our heart. What kind of "trash"? First of all, the trash mentioned in Ephesians 4:31. "Let all bitterness, and wrath, and anger, and clamour, and evil speaking, be put away from you, with all malice." Also, let us throw out "all malice, and all guile, and hypocrisies, and envies, and all evil speakings," (First Peter 2:1)

According to the results of a survey conducted by the Japan National Cancer Center, a person can improve his health by 14% by quitting one of these habits: tobacco, alcohol, using too much salt, and overeating. Likewise, a Christian can improve his spiritual condition by throwing out all the "trash" in his heart.

NINE THOUSAND YEN FOR
FIVE MINUTES OF WORK

—✧—

I bought a wireless notebook computer. I can use it in any room, so it is quite convenient. However, a couple of days after I bought it, suddenly I could not connect to the Internet any longer. I contacted the provider and asked them to send someone to repair it.

After looking at my computer for just five minutes, the repairman turned one switch from OFF to ON and the problem was solved. He explained, "Because we made a house call, the cost will be nine thousand yen ($90).

However, since it took only five minutes, I will call the office and see if they will make it cheaper." The office listened to his explanation that the repair only took five minutes, but they told him, "No, we cannot make it cheaper. The cost for a house call is nine thousand yen," so I had to pay nine thousand yen for just five minutes of work.

The small switch that was turned OFF is not as important as the hard disk or mother board, but as long as it is OFF, the computer is useless.

In Second Timothy 2:20-21 it is written, "In a great house there are not only vessels of gold and of silver, but also of wood and of earth; and some to honour, and some to dishonour. If a man therefore purge himself from these, he shall be a vessel unto honour, sanctified, and meet for the master's use, and prepared unto every good work."

When each member becomes a vessel that can be used by the Lord, the church becomes a church that is prepared to every good work. From time to time, let's examine ourselves and see if we are OFF or ON. In other words, in our present condition, are we a vessel meet for the Master's use?

NO FISH

On the second day of the Nagashima Camp we went fishing. Pastor Kishimoto, Pastor Miyake and his wife caught at least one fish. The young people all caught at least one fish. Even the children, Ethan, Kayla and Yuki caught at least one fish.

There was only one person who did not catch at least one fish. Yep, I was that person. The sea was clear that day, so I could see many fish, but even if I dropped my hook right in the middle of a crowd of fish, the bait was quickly stolen. I may be the worst fisherman in the world. Since childhood, I have loved fishing, but I have yet to figure out an effective method of catching fish.

The Bible compares evangelism to fishing. In Matthew 4:19 Jesus said to His disciples, "Follow me, and I will make you fishers of men." All Christians have been commissioned to declare the gospel in various ways and fish for men. I do not know how to catch fish, but I know how to catch men.

In John 15:5 Jesus said, "He that abideth in me, and I in him, the same bringeth forth much fruit: for without me ye can do nothing." This passage compares evangelism to bearing fruit, so even if we read it like this, the meaning does not change: "He that abideth in me, and I in him, the same will catch many men."

The secret of the Christian fisherman who wants to catch many men is abiding in Christ. It is not a problem of how skillful a fisherman we are. If you have been fishing for men with little or no results, try spending some time each day in fellowship with Christ.

NO MONKEYS

Last Monday I took Missionary Dan Gardner, the guest speaker for our special meeting at the Kokura church, to Beppu. I intended to take him to Mount Takasaki where many monkeys live, to the Umitamago Aquarium and to the area called Hell where there are many hot springs. However, when we arrived at the parking lot, we were told, "The monkeys have not come out yet, so go to the aquarium first."

We went to the aquarium and then went to see if the monkeys had come out, but there was not one monkey anywhere. We waited a while, but not one monkey appeared. Usually there are over one hundred monkeys walking around freely. I wanted Brother Gardner to see them, so I was quite disappointed.

Our experience was similar to the experience of many Christians. They pray to the Lord and wait expectantly for His answer, but when He does not answer right away, they are disappointed. Psalm 27:14 tells us what to do when this happens. "Wait on the Lord: be of good courage, and he shall strengthen thine heart: wait, I say, on the Lord."

I have been to Mount Takasaki many times and until now, the monkeys have always come out, but this time they disappointed me. However, the Lord will never disappoint us, so let's remember the words in Isaiah 40:31 and keep on praying. "They that wait upon the Lord shall renew their strength; they shall mount up with wings as eagles; they shall run, and not be weary; and they shall walk, and not faint."

Are you discouraged because something you eagerly expected did not materialize? Do not despair. When the time is right, the Lord will answer.

NO ONE WOULD ANSWER!

The first night of Summer Camp I warned everyone. "One of the main purposes of Camp is fellowship, so before you leave your room in the morning, turn off your I-pad, smart phone, and cell phone. If I see you using any of these devices outside your room, I will take them away and not return them until Camp is over."

The next morning, one of the young ladies hurt her foot, so I had to go to the hospital with her and her parents. We didn't have an appointment, so we had to wait quite a while. After we were finally finished, I thought I would call and let everyone know that we were on our way back.

First, I called Brother Yamaguchi, but he didn't answer. Next, I called Brother Koh, but he didn't answer. Finally, I called Mrs. Yamaguchi, but she didn't answer. No one would answer!

When I returned to Camp, I asked them, "Why didn't you answer your phone?" Their replies made me laugh. "We were afraid you would take away our phones, so we turned them off." I had been irritated because no one would answer his phone, but at the same time, I was happy that they had heeded my warning.

The pastor is always happy when church members heed his warnings, but he is even happier when they heed the warnings of the Lord. For example, are you heeding this warning? "Watch and pray, that ye enter not into temptation: the spirit indeed is willing, but the flesh is weak." (Matthew 26:41) How about this one? "Take heed, and beware of covetousness: for a man's life consisteth not in the abundance of the things which he possesseth." (Luke 12:15)

NOT EVEN IN HEAVEN

The first day of my trip to Taiwan, Pastor Sakai and several Christians took me to a restaurant. It was a fantastic meal. I ate *shumai*, duck, shrimp, fish, noodles, watermelon, tapioca, and sesame seed dumplings. I ate several other foods, but this is all I can remember.

The food was so delicious, I jokingly said, "There isn't food this delicious anywhere, not even in heaven." Everyone laughed, but one lady replied to me with these words, "If that is true, "I do not want to go to heaven." Everyone laughed even louder.

She said it jokingly, but she was right. No matter how luxurious our life may be on this earth, our life in heaven will be even more luxurious. The meal I ate in Taiwan was quite delicious, but it does not compare to our meal in heaven, for according to Revelation 19:9, we are invited to the marriage supper of the Lamb. Also, in Matthew 8:11 Jesus said, "Many shall come from the east and west, and shall sit down with Abraham, and Isaac, and Jacob, in the kingdom of heaven." Imagine the meal we shall eat! It will be far more delicious than anything we have ever eaten on earth.

The most delicious drink there is on earth cannot compare to what we will drink in heaven, for we shall drink the "water of life, clear as crystal." (Revelation 22:1)

Often, I hear people say, "It can't get any better than this." Oh yes it can! "Eye hath not seen, nor ear heard, neither have entered into the heart of man, the things which God hath prepared for them that love him." (First Corinthians 2:9)

NOW HE CAN SEE

Somewhere around 1982 another pastor asked me if I would like to help start a new church. I agreed, so one day he took me to the town of Amagi. There I met Brother and Sister Inamoto for the first time. Both of them were blind.

Brother Inamoto worked as an acupuncturist in a room in his home. We decided to begin a weekly Bible study at his house. We gathered around the table he used for his work on Sunday nights and Thursday nights. This was the beginning of my 38-years-long fellowship with Brother Inamoto. The people who went to the Bible study changed many times, but until a pastor came to the Amagi church, I drove an hour and a half to Amagi two times a week.

He could play the flute so skillfully that many times I wept as I listened to him play.

Last week Brother Inamoto went home to be with the Lord. Now he can see. He and his wife, who had already gone home to be with the Lord, were able to see each other's face for the first time.

How wonderful is the place that God is preparing for everyone who believes in Jesus Christ! "Then the eyes of the blind shall be opened, and the ears of the deaf shall be unstopped. Then shall the lame man leap as an hart, and the tongue of the dumb sing: for in the wilderness shall waters break out, and streams in the desert." (Isaiah 35:5-6)

What a glorious day that will be when one day I see Brother Inamoto and Sister Inamoto in Heaven!

NUMBER 21

Once a month I have to be examined by a urologist. The first time I went to his office, I was made to wait three and one-half hours! When I am made to wait a long time, I become irritated, so from then on, I went at seven o'clock in the morning and signed in. When I did that, I was usually sixth or seventh in line.

However, from this month, the clinic opens not at seven o'clock but at eight o'clock. Thinking I would be near the head of the line, I went at 7:45. However, I found a crowd of people waiting at the front door. Instead of being sixth or seventh, I was number 21, so again I had to wait a long time.

In America, both large hospitals and small clinics use the appointment system, so usually we do not have to wait very long. Because of my impatient personality, I think the appointment system of America is much better than the first-come first-serve system of Japan.

Actually, there is a system that is superior to systems of both America and Japan. It is the system of God who responds to our prayers for help. We do not have to make appointments, nor do we have to line up behind many other people. God never says, "Your appointment to talk with me is two o'clock tomorrow afternoon, so wait until then," or "You are number 21 in line, so wait until I hear the prayers of the 20 people in front of you."

David wrote this testimony in Psalm 18:6: "In my distress I called upon the Lord, and cried unto my God: he heard my voice out of his temple, and my cry came before him, even into his ears."

NUMBERS! NUMBERS! I HATE NUMBERS!

When I went to the church the other day, there was a notice in the mailbox that the deliveryman had delivered a package, but since no one was there, I needed to call the post office and set up a time to have it delivered when someone would be at the church. (In Japan, the deliveryman cannot just leave the package on the porch. He has to hand it to a person.)

I called the number on the notice and followed the instructions of the recorded message: Telephone number. Zip code. Number of the notice. What kind of package? Day and time of delivery. It went well this far, but I did not understand the next instruction, so I put in the wrong number and had to start all over again.

Telephone number. Zip code. Number of the notice. What kind of package? Day and time of delivery. Once again, I misunderstood the instructions and made a mistake. I angrily slammed the phone down and yelled, "Numbers! Numbers! Numbers! I hate numbers. I want to talk with a human being!" I finally gave up and had one of the church members make the call for me.

Imagine praying to God and having a machine answer and ask for the following information: Name. Birthday. Address. The day you became a Christian. The day you were baptized. The name of the church where you attend. This would be terrible. I would shout, "I want to talk to God.!"

Happily, when we pray to the Lord, the Lord Himself answers. "In the day of my trouble I will call upon thee: for thou wilt answer me." (Psalm 86:7)

NUREGINU (WET CLOTHES)

I heard an interesting story from a lady who comes to my English class. There was a war lord who lived with his wife and extremely beautiful daughter. One day the wife died. Later, the war lord remarried. However, because the daughter was so beautiful, the war lord's new wife hated her.

One night, when her stepdaughter was sleeping, the stepmother crept into the room and laid the wet clothes of a fisherman near her stepdaughter's bed. When the war lord found the wet clothes the next morning, he mistakenly thought his daughter was having an affair with the fisherman. He became angry and killed her.

Out of this story came the expression *nureginu o kiseru*. which literally means "to put wet clothes on someone." The real meaning of the word as it is used today is "to accuse someone falsely."

When I heard this story, I immediately remembered the story of Christ. The Bible declares that Christ did not commit even one sin. (Hebrews 4:15) When the Roman government held the trial of Christ, a governor named Pilate conducted the investigation. His verdict is written three times in chapter 23 of Luke's Gospel. "I find no fault in this man." (Verse 4) "I, having examined him before you, have found no fault in this man." (Verse 14) "I have found no cause for death in him." (Verse 22)

It is true. Christ was sinless. They "put wet clothes" on Christ. When He died on the cross, He died not for His own sins but for our sins. "Who his own self bare our sins in his own body on the tree, that we, being dead to sins, should live unto righteousness: by whose stripes ye were healed." (First Peter 2:24)

OH NO! I DROPPED JESUS!

During the month of December, we place a display of the birth of Christ in front of the church almost every night. There are statues of Mary and Joseph and a doll representing Jesus in a manger.

When we were setting up the display the Sunday before Christmas, there was an unexpected happening. I carried the statues of Joseph and Mary safely to the display and went back to get the manger and baby Jesus. As I was walking to the door carrying the manger with baby Jesus in it, my foot slipped, and to keep from falling, I dropped the manger. When the manger hit the floor, baby Jesus fell off the manger and began rolling across the parking lot. Of course, it was just a doll, but I exclaimed, "Oh no! I dropped Jesus!"

It was not the first time I had "dropped" Jesus. During my 56 years as a Christian, I have "dropped" Jesus many times. In other words, my feet have slipped on sin and I have done things that were not pleasing to the Lord. My experience was the same as the experience of David. "But as for me, my feet were almost gone; my steps had well nigh slipped." (Psalm 73:2)

There have been times when my feet too have well nigh slipped; however, I can give this testimony. Jesus has never dropped me even one time. I have disappointed the Lord, but He has never disappointed me.

The words of a well-known hymn sum up my Christian life:

Jesus never fails, Jesus never fails
Heaven and earth may pass away
But Jesus never fails.

ONE DOOR

———— ❧ ————

There is a famous hot springs called Bessho near the town of Ueda in Nagano Prefecture. It is one of the oldest hot springs in Japan and the oldest one in Nagano. It said that the water of Bessho makes the skin beautiful, so Bessho is a favorite hot spring of many women.

A train that runs from the town of Ueda to Bessho is popular with many people. The train only runs the seven miles between Ueda and Bessho. When I went to preach at a church in Ueda, I rode this train on the way to the church.

When the train stopped at my station, I was surprised. Different than most trains that have many doors, this train had only one door. I had to walk all the way from the back of the train to the front to get off.

As I walked from the station to the church, I pondered the words of Christ in John 10:9. "I am the door: by me if any man enter in, he shall be saved."

Some people try to enter heaven through the door of good works, but according to Ephesians 2:8-9, no one can enter heaven by his good works.

Some people try to enter heaven by ceremonies such as baptism; however, in First Peter 3:21 the Bible teaches that baptism is "not the putting away of the filth of the flesh."

The door to heaven is not good works nor religious ceremonies; It is a person. Jesus said, "I am the door," In John 14:6 Jesus said, "I am the way, the truth, and the life: no man cometh unto the Father, but by me." ONE DOOR!

ONE DROP OF KETCHUP

On the way to Sasebo, I went through the drive-thru at McDonald's and bought a hamburger. As I drove along enjoying the hamburger, suddenly a drop of ketchup fell on my white shirt. I quickly grabbed a tissue and tried to wipe it off, but the stain just got bigger and bigger.

That night I was supposed to attend a service at a church in Sasebo. But that's not all. The next day, I had to go to a funeral. Not only that, I would have to stand up in front of everyone with the ketchup stain on my white shirt and deliver the message at the funeral.

I did not have enough time to go home, so I went into a convenience store, bought some cleanser, went into the bathroom and used the cleanser to wipe off the stain. I was able to wipe off some of it, but there was still a big stain. When I went to church that night, I tried to hide the stain by pulling my necktie as far to the right as possible and keeping my coat buttoned.

The image of me trying to hide the stain on my shirt is the image of many people trying to hide the "stain" of sin on their hearts. Through religion or good works or a nice outward appearance, they are trying to hide their sins from God and other people, but even if they are able to hide them from other people, they cannot hide them from God. "Man looketh on the outward appearance, but the Lord looketh on the heart." (First Samuel 16:7)

Instead of trying to hide our sins, let's openly confess our sins to the Lord and pray the same prayer that the publican prayed in Luke 18:13. "God be merciful to me a sinner."

ONE, TWO, ONE, TWO

When I was young, I could distribute hundreds of tracts and flyers in a day without getting tired. Now, I am 75 years old and I get tired after distributing just 100 flyers. In addition, because of the nerve pain in my feet, they begin to hurt after just a few minutes.

I distributed some flyers the other day and, sure enough, when I finished, I was very tired and my feet were hurting. Not only that, it was quite a distance back to my car. Fatigued and in pain, I slowly walked toward the car.

Finally, I reached the place where I could see my car in the distance. I did not feel like taking another step, but I fixed my eyes on my car and saying over and over again, "One, two, one two," I managed to make it to the car one step at a time,

There are times when the Christian will have a similar experience. His heart is hurting because of some unexpected event and he thinks, "I cannot go any further."

When the Christian life becomes this kind of laborious life, just as I walked one step at a time saying, "One, two, one two," let's pray, "Lord, give me the strength to walk one more step. Give me the strength to live one more day."

In Philippians 3:13-14 Paul wrote, "This one thing I do, forgetting those things which are behind, and reaching forth unto those things which are before, I press toward the <u>mark</u> for the prize of the high calling of God in Christ Jesus." One step at a time. One, two, one, two,

"ONIONS MIXED IN TURPENTINE"

Have you ever eaten the durian fruit? People who have eaten durians say that the smell of the durian is like the smell of "onions mixed in turpentine." I had never eaten durian, but one of the church members who had recently visited Thailand brought some durian to church and shared it with everyone during lunch. Before he gave us the present, he said, "This has a little bit of a smell." A couple of the church members smelled it and said, "It smells like propane gas."

I took it and smelled it, but because my sense of smell is very dull, I could not smell anything. Several of the church members declined the fruit because of its smell, but I took some and ate it. It was delicious.

The smell of the fruit was unpleasant to everyone, but the smell of the love of the brother who brought it to us was a sweet-smelling fragrance. In his letter to the Philippians, Paul wrote, "I have all, and abound: I am full, having received of Epaphroditus the things which were sent from you, an odour of a sweet smell, a sacrifice acceptable, wellpleasing to God."

The love of Christ for us was a fragrant love too. "Christ also hath loved us, and hath given himself for us an offering and a sacrifice to God for a sweetsmelling savour." (Ephesians 5:2) In those days, death by the cross was the most unpleasant death, but to us who were saved from the penalty of sin by the cross, the fragrance of the cross is a sweet-smelling fragrance.

Ephesians 5:1-2 teaches us the proper response to the fragrant love of Christ. "Be ye therefore followers of God, as dear children And walk in love."

ONLY FOUR POSTCARDS

(The Japanese do not send Christmas cards, but there is a custom to send New Year postcards. Although I adopted many of the customs of Japan, I chose to ignore this custom.)

How many New Year postcards did you receive? I received only four. One of those was from my son and the other three were from the company that cleans my house, my insurance company and my doctor.

I received only one personal New Year postcard because I do not send New Year postcards. It makes sense. The person who does not send postcards will not receive any postcards. This principle aligns with what is called the "law of the harvest" written in Second Corinthians 9:6. "He which soweth sparingly shall reap also sparingly; and he which soweth bountifully shall reap also bountifully."

Of course, this is an agricultural principle. No matter what kind of vegetable or fruit it may be, the person who desires a bountiful harvest must sow many seeds.

We can apply this principle to all facets of life. The person who desires friends must make an effort to draw close to others. The person who wishes others to be kind to him must show kindness to others. The person who is seeking love must give love to others. The person who wants to be blessed should strive to be a blessing to others.

There is a famous Bible passage that sums up the "law of the harvest." It is the passage called "the golden rule" written in Luke 6:31. "As ye would that men should do to you, do ye also to them likewise."

ONLY 0.02%

———— ❧ ————

Do you have a My Number card (a personal number card provided for all Japanese)? It is said that only 13% of the people have the My Number cards that were issued four years ago.

There is a My Number Portal for all people who have a My Number card. Three services are provided for people who log into the Portal: 1-You can check and see how government agencies are using your personal information. 2-You can confirm payments you have made for taxes and health insurance. 3-You can hear announcements concerning preventative vaccinations.

Even though these services are available, it is said that only 0.02% of the people who have My Number cards are taking advantage of the My Number Portal.

Many Christians too are not taking advantage of the many promises God has provided. For example, are we taking advantage of the following promises?

The promise concerning offerings (Malachi 3:10)
The promise concerning the desire of our heart (Psalm 37:4)
The promise concerning prayer (Philippians 4:6-7)
The promise concerning guidance (Proverbs 3:5-6)
The promise concerning daily necessities (Matthew 6:31-33)

A My Promise Portal has been provided for everyone who believes in Christ. I wonder if only 0.02% of Christians are taking advantage of this great opportunity.

OUR BATTLE WITH THE GIANT WEED

When the church moved to the new location, we found a giant weed right outside the back door. It was so big that, when we cleaned up the back yard, we just cut off the part that was above ground and ignored the root.

Last Sunday, I became tired of looking at that ugly weed and decided to dig it up. Brother Koh and Sister Kaoru saw me trying to dig it up and came to help me. The more we dug, the more we found tangled roots. Twice I became dizzy and had to go inside the church and rest for a while, but Brother Koh and Sister Kaoru continued the battle. It took quite a while, but we were finally able to dig up all the roots.

As I watched Brother Koh and Sister Kaoru battle with the giant weed, I could see the image of people who are battling with sins that have spread roots deep into their hearts. Knowing that their actions are sins, they deceive themselves with thoughts such as, "Just a little bit won't hurt. I'll be all right."

However, the more they continue those actions, the more the roots spread deeper and deeper into their hearts and eventually control their way of living and way of thinking. When they finally realize the influence of their sins, they try to dig them out, but the roots are tangled too deep into their hearts.

When God shows us our sins, let's stop them before they become a giant weed. "Wherefore seeing we also are compassed about with so great a cloud of witnesses, let us lay aside every weight, and <u>the sin which doth so easily beset us</u>, and let us run with patience the race that is set before us." (Hebrews 12:1)

OUR LAST MEAL

— ❧ —

After coming to Japan, my wife and I learned to love *gyooza* (meat dumplings), so she quickly learned how to make *gyooza*. However, the *gyooza* she made was different from the *gyooza* you buy at stores or order in restaurants. It had lots of meat in it. I often enjoyed my wife's delicious *gyooza*. In fact, the last meal she prepared for me was *gyooza*. I still eat *gyooza* once in a while and think of my wife and her delicious *gyooza* as I eat it.

Today we shall observe the Lord's Supper. The night before He was crucified, Jesus ate a meal with His disciples. "And as they did eat, Jesus took bread, and blessed, and brake it, and gave to them, and said, Take, eat: this is my body. And he took the cup, and when he had given thanks, he gave it to them: and they all drank of it. And he said unto them, This is my blood of the new testament, which is shed for many." (Mark 14:22-24) The famous artist, Da Vinci, brilliantly captured this scene in his famous painting, "The Last Supper."

What is the purpose of this observance called "The Lord's Supper"? First Corinthians 11:23-26 teaches us that purpose. Paul quotes Christ in this passage. According to Christ's own words, the purpose of the observance of the Lord's Supper is to show forth His death. (verse 26)

Just as I remember my wife and her last meal whenever I eat *gyooza*, whenever we partake of the bread and the grape juice, let's remember the great sacrifice that Christ paid to redeem us – the scarred body and the precious blood that Jesus shed to cleanse our sinful hearts. "Foreasmuch as ye know that ye were not redeemed with corruptible things, . . . But with the precious blood of Christ." (First Peter 1:18-19)

PASS CARD

A few days before the JBBF National Camp, everyone received this email: You will receive a "pass card" (a name tag to be worn on a string around the neck). If you do not have your pass card, you will not be allowed to enter the auditorium.

I wore the pass card for the first two services, but I decided to test the rule before the third service. I hid the pass card in my pocket and tried to enter the auditorium, but I was stopped at the entrance. "Pastor Board, where is your pass card?" I pulled it out of my pocket and showed it to him. He said, "Please put it around your neck."

When I tried to enter the auditorium for the final service, again I was stopped. "Pastor Board, you cannot enter without your pass card." I replied, "But I am the speaker for this service." With a chagrinned look on his face he said, "Go on in." Laughing, I pulled my pass card out of my pocket and showed it to him.

The email read, "If you do not have your pass card, you will not be allowed to enter the auditorium," but because I was the speaker, I was allowed to enter without a pass card. However, the person who does not obey the "rule" for entering heaven, no matter who it is, will not be allowed into heaven. What is that "rule"?

"Except a man be born again, he cannot see the kingdom of God." (John 3:3) "Except a man be born of water and of the Spirit, he cannot enter into the kingdom of God." (John 3:5) We are "born again" through faith in Jesus Christ who died for our sins. Faith in Him is the pass card for entrance into heaven.

PICTURE BOOK OF HELL

Have you ever read *The Picture Book of Hell*? It was published in 1980. In this book there are many vivid illustrations of Hell. For example, there is a picture of people being thrown into a pot of boiling water.

This book which was published thirty-two years ago has recently been selling well. Akiko Higashimura wrote a comic book about her problems in raising her son. One day, in order to persuade her son to become a better child, she showed him *The Picture Book of Hell*. It worked. He became a more well-mannered son. Now many mothers are using that book as a method of raising obedient children.

There are no pictures of Hell in the Bible, but there are many passages that teach the existence of Hell. Hell is a place where people cry and gnash their teeth. (Matthew 25:30) Hell is a place where people suffer in flames. (Luke 16:23-24) Hell is a place where people find no rest night and day. (Revelation 14:11) The passage that especially teaches the horror of Hell is Revelation 21:8. "The fearful, and unbelieving, and the abominable, and murderers, and whoremongers, and sorcerers, and idolaters, and all liars, shall have their part in the lake which burneth with fire and brimstone: which is the second death."

The actual Hell is much more horrible than the Hell pictured in *The Picture Book of Hell*. However, according to the Bible, it is not the desire of God for even one person to go to Hell. "The Lord is not slack concerning his promise, as some men count slackness; but is longsuffering to us-ward, not willing that any should perish, but that all should come to repentance." (Second Peter 3:9) God made it possible for everyone to avoid Hell by sending His own Son to die on the cross for us. (John 3:16)

"PLEASE CHANGE THIS WATER INTO COCA-COLA"

⟡

A typhoon was headed my way. A friend told me, "Pastor, it is a powerful typhoon. You may not have any water tomorrow, so you had better be prepared." I found five large Coca-Cola bottles and filled them with water.

After the typhoon, I still had water, so I wondered what to do with the five bottles of water. Then I remembered the miracle that Jesus performed in chapter two of the Gospel of John. Jesus turned water into wine. I know that the Lord still performs miracles, so I prayed, "Lord, please change this water into Coca-Cola." I have been waiting for five days, but the water is still water.

You may laugh at my foolishness, but my prayer resembles the prayer of many people who pray self-centered prayers without any thought of the will of God.

Certainly, you remember the prayer that Jesus taught His disciples, the prayer that is called "The Lord's Prayer." If we make that prayer our example, before we ask for anything, we should pray, "Thy will be done in earth, as it is in heaven." In other words, before we say our requests to the Lord, we should consider whether our requests are the will of the Lord or not. If we do not seek the will of the Lord before we pray, our prayers will probably end up like my "Please change this water into Coca-Cola" prayer.

"And this is the confidence that we have in him, that, if we ask any thing according to his will, he heareth us:" (First John 5:14) I wonder, are you waiting for the Lord to answer a prayer that is not His will?

KEN BOARD

PROOF OF INSPECTION

My neighbor asked me, "Did you get your car inspected?" I replied, "Yes." Then he asked, "Where is the certificate that you place on your windshield? If you do not have that, you may be stopped by the police and have to pay a fine."

I remember receiving the certificate, but when I searched my home and my briefcase, I could not find it. Finally, I found it in the glove compartment of my car. Although I did have the certificate, because it was not in a place where it could be seen, no one could know if I had the certificate or not.

The Epistle of James teaches us that the same principle applies to our faith. Although we may have faith in our heart, if there are no outward works that prove our faith, others will not be able to know that we are Christians.

"Yea, a man may say, Thou hast faith, and I have works: shew me thy faith without thy works, and I will shew thee my faith by my works." (James 2:18)

We may confess our faith in Jesus Christ to our family and friends, but if there are no works that can be seen by them, there is a strong possibility that they may doubt the veracity of our faith. When a Christian obeys the teachings of the Bible, his works are like an inspection certificate placed on the windshield of a car.

"Let your light so shine before men, that they may see your good works, and glorify your Father which is in heaven." (Matthew 5:16)

"PULL THE PLUG"

The message on the screen said, "This page cannot be viewed." I tried several times, but the message was the same every time. I could not get into the Internet. I know almost nothing about computers, so I called my provider and explained the situation. His answer surprised me. "Pull the plug."

I said, "Pull the plug?" He replied, "Yes. Pull all the plugs connecting the computer and the router." I asked, "All of them?" He said, "Yes, pull all the plugs, wait ten seconds and plug them back in." When I did exactly what he told me to do, I was able to get back into the Internet.

The solution to the problem was to pull the plug. The method of solving many of the problems of the heart is the same method. We must pull the plug on our busy life and, through prayer and the Bible, spend some time with the Lord.

"In the morning, rising up a great while before day, he went out, and departed into a solitary place, and there prayed." (Mark 1:35) "He withdrew himself into the wilderness, and prayed." (Luke 5:16) If Jesus felt it was important to pull the plug on His busy life and spend time in prayer, how much more important is it for us to spend time alone with God!

When I pulled all the plugs, I was able to solve my computer problem in 10 seconds. When we are struggling with problems of the heart, problems which we cannot solve ourselves, if we pulled the plug on our busy life, separated ourselves from the affairs of this world and spent time with the Lord, we could solve our problems in about 10 minutes.

RAMEN JIRO

When I went to Tokyo, Pastor Saitoh told me about a ramen shop called Ramen Jiro. We did not have time to go there on Thursday or Friday, but finally we went there for lunch on Saturday.

When we arrived at the shop, I was surprised at two things. First, I was surprised at the size of the shop. It was a small shop that could seat only thirteen customers. Second, I was surprised at the popularity of the shop. People were lined up outside. Pastor Saitoh and I stood in line about thirty minutes. While we were waiting, he explained the method of ordering to me. Before sitting at the counter, we had to decide the following things:

Size (small or large)
Noodles (regular or hard)
Vegetables (yes or no)
Garlic (none, a little, regular, double)

Before sitting at the counter, I rehearsed my order over and over: (small, regular, vegetables, a little). The ramen I ate that day was a very delicious ramen just right for my taste.

The method of ordering your meal at that shop resembles the right way of praying. Perhaps we do not receive what we desire from the Lord because our prayers are too ambiguous. When Jesus said to Bartimaeus, "What wilt thou that I should do unto thee?" Bartimaeus replied specifically, "Lord, that I might receive my sight." (Mark 10:51)

Before we kneel to pray, let's decide what we want to "order."

RESURRECTION VICTORY

In 2015 Terunofuji won the summer sumo tournament. Everyone was certain he would become the next grand champion. However, he was struggling with diabetes and hepatitis and had surgery on both knees. After the surgery, he returned to sumo, but he no longer had as much power as before, so he fell from the rank of champion to the rank of 48 in the lowest division of sumo. No sumo wrestler had ever fallen that far before. (For Americans who do not understand sumo rankings, this would be comparable to the MVP of major league baseball falling all the way to Class A in the minor leagues.)

He considered retirement several times, but he slowly regained his power and fought his way back into the upper division of sumo. In last month's tournament, in a match that moved many sumo fans to tears, he won the championship. They are calling his victory a "resurrection victory."

Certainly, his victory was an impressive victory, but there is an even more impressive "resurrection victory." It is the resurrection victory of Jesus Christ. After He was crucified, His body was placed in a tomb. However, on the third day He arose from the dead. "Christ died for our sins according to the scriptures; And that he was buried, and that he rose again the third day according to the scriptures." (First Corinthians 15:3-4)

Christ entered the tomb, fought with death and won the victory. Therefore, in First Corinthians 15:55 it is written, "O death, where is thy sting? O grave, where is thy victory?" In verse 57 there are words that remove the fear of death from every Christian. "Thanks be to God, which giveth us the victory through our Lord Jesus Christ."

ROAD CLOSED! ROAD CLOSED!

An extremely strong typhoon arrived in Kitakyushu City the last day of Summer Camp. Two of the campers had planned to return to Fukuoka City by train, but the trains were not running, so I offered to drive them.

I decided to take the City Expressway, but when I arrived at the entrance, there was a "Road Closed" sign. I changed my plan and headed for the Kyushu Expressway, but when I arrived at the entrance, there was a "Road Closed" sign, so I had to take the regular highway.

It was the same on the way home. When I tried to return by the Kyushu Expressway and the City Expressway, the "Road Closed" signs were still there, so I had to drive all the way home on crowded highways. A trip that should have taken two hours took five hours.

Sometimes there are "Road Closed" signs in the life of a Christian. We intend to follow the leadership of the Lord, but suddenly there is a "Road Closed" sign in our path. What should we do when this happens?

Do as I did. Look for an open road. Usually, when the Lord closes one road, He opens a different road. God closes one road in order to lead us to the right road, a road that is much safer. The most famous example of this is Missionary David Livingstone. He intended to go to China, but the road was closed because of a war, so he went to Africa.

When we see a "Road Closed" sign, let's follow the words in Proverbs 3:5-6. "Trust in the Lord with all thine heart; and lean not unto thine own understanding. In all thy ways acknowledge him, and he shall direct thy paths."

RUN FOR THE MONEY

—— ❧ ——

While I was in Kagoshima, I watched a very interesting TV program with my son and his family. It was a program called "Run for the Money." The program took place in a large shopping mall. The participants were twenty people from the world of entertainment and sports.

For 130 minutes they have to escape from three "hunters." If they are captured, they receive no money. If they can manage to evade the hunters for 130 minutes, they receive $7,800 (one dollar for each second).

During the program, the participants have to carry out various "missions." If they are unable to carry out the mission in the allotted time, the number of "hunters" increase. During the program I became quite excited and yelled, "Look out! Hurry up and escape!"

As I was watching the program, I thought, "This program resembles the Christian life." According to First Peter 5:8, there is a "hunter" who is pursuing Christians. "Be sober, be vigilant; because your adversary the devil, as a roaring lion, walketh about, seeking whom he may devour." We are exhorted to do two things so we will not be captured by this "hunter." Be sober and be vigilant.

While I was watching this program, I noticed one more thing. The participants had to cooperate to carry out the missions. Two to three participants were necessary to carry out each mission. In order for the church to carry out the mission that Christ gave to it, the cooperation of each member is necessary. The church in Jerusalem is our example. The words in Acts 2:42 explain the success of their evangelism. "The multitude of them that believed were of one heart and of one soul."

SEARCHING FOR HER DAUGHTER

Three months have passed since the massive earthquake and tidal wave. According to a June 14th newspaper article, 7,391 people are still missing. One of those is a three-year-old girl name Yu Miura. When the tidal wave washed their home away, she died along with her father, grandfather, and grandmother. The bodies of her father, grandfather, and grandmother have been recovered, but the body of Yu has not been found yet.

The mother of Yu was in another town on the day of the tragedy. It took her three days to return home. Every day she searches for her daughter. She fears that the body of Yu will be carried away with the rubble, so she warns those clearing the rubble to be careful.

She vowed, "I will do everything possible to find my daughter." One day when she was searching, she saw a butterfly and remembered something her daughter had said. "When I get big, I want to be a butterfly." When she saw the butterfly, she vowed, "I will not leave here until I see my daughter again."

When I read the article about the vow of the mother of Yu, these questions troubled me: "Am I searching for lost souls as passionately as this mother who is searching for her daughter? Am I doing all I can to search for lost souls?"

Also, as I thought of this mother searching for her daughter, I thought of the Savior, Jesus Christ, who left heaven and came to our world to search for us. "For the Son of man is come to seek and to save that which was lost." (Luke 19:10)

SHE COULN'T EAT HER OWN CAKE

Three of the church members had birthdays in May, so last week one of the ladies made a very delicious birthday cake for them. The icing was chocolate and the color of the cake was green and pink, so we called it a "Rainbow Cake."

Except for one person, everyone ate some cake. That one person was the lady who made the cake. She cannot eat anything that has gluten in it. One of the ladies said to her, "It's too bad. You made the cake, but you can't eat it."

The instant I heard her words, I remembered the words of mockery hurled at Christ by His enemies. "He saved others; himself he cannot save." (Matthew 27:42)

Actually, He could have saved Himself. In Matthew 26:53 when one of His disciples drew a sword and tried to save Him, He said, "Thinkest thou that I cannot now pray to my Father, and he shall presently give me more than twelve legions of angels?"

Yes, Christ could have easily saved Himself, but He chose not to do so. Why? "For Christ also hath once suffered for sins, the just for the unjust, that he might bring us to God." (First Peter 3:18)

There is another reason why Christ did not save Himself. "Who his own self bare our sins in his own body on the tree, that we, being dead to sins, should live unto righteousness: by whose stripes ye were healed.." (First Peter 2:24) Because He chose to die to save us from our sins, let us choose to die to sin and live a righteous life.

SHIMONOSEKI AND SHIMOSONE EKI

In chapter twelve of Judges there is the account of the Ephraimites who could not pronounce the word "Shibboleth" correctly.

I too have some words that are hard to pronounce. There is a city near me called Shimonoseki. The train station nearest to my home is called Shimosone Eki. For some reason, these two names are difficult for me to pronounce correctly. Sometimes I even combine them into one word. Recently, when I wanted to go to the train station, I told the taxi driver to take me to "Shimosonenoseki." The driver, with a confused look on his face said, "Where?"

There are some words that are difficult for all people to say. It is hard for us to say, "I am a sinner," or "I have sinned." Why is it so difficult for us to admit our sins? I suppose the admission that we have sinned hurts our pride.

According to First John 1:10, the person who is not willing to admit, "I have sinned," commits the grave sin of making God a liar. "If we say that we have not sinned, we make him a liar, and his word is not in us."

If we can overcome our pride and admit our sins, what will happen? "He that covereth his sins shall not prosper: but whoso confesseth and forsaketh them shall have mercy." (Proverbs 28:13)

"I am a sinner." Try saying these words to the Lord. "If we confess our sins, he is faithful and just to forgive us our sins, and to cleanse us from all unrighteousness." (First John 1:9)

SHOOTEN

Usually, when I watch TV, I watch shows in English, but there is one Japanese show that I really like. It is a show called *Shooten* that is similar to the American Program *Whose Line Is It Anyway*, except that the contestants are sitting on cushions. When they give answers that please the moderator, they are awarded more cushions; however, when their answers displease him, he takes away a cushion. When one of the contestants accumulates ten cushions, he wins a prize.

I think *Enraku* is the most clever contestant. If he always gave clever answers, he could accumulate ten cushions quickly; however, he deliberately gives answers that displease the moderator, so he often loses all of his cushions. In a recent show, his answer so upset the moderator that he took away the cushions of all the contestants.

When I saw that, I thought of a principle taught in the Bible. It is the principle that our actions and words have an influence on other people. There is a famous illustration of this principle in chapter seven of Joshua. As a result of the sin of a man named Achan, thirty-seven Israeli soldiers were killed in battle. In addition, God poured out His anger on the entire congregation. "Did not Achan the son of Zerah commit a trespass in the accursed thing, and wrath fell on all the congregation of Israel? and that man perished not alone in his iniquity."

The actions of a careless driver, an unfaithful husband or wife, or the reckless life of a child can have a devastating effect on many other people. When the answers of *Enraku* cause all of the other contestants to lose their cushions too, I think it is hilarious; however, when our deeds and words bring harm to others, it is no laughing matter.

SHOUTS OF JOY AT SIX
IN THE MORNING

It was just a little before six in the morning. I was drinking coffee and reading some email. Suddenly I heard shouts of joy coming from several homes in the neighborhood. I wondered, "Why are people shouting for joy at this time in the morning?" After considering what it could be, I realized it was a World Cup soccer match. The neighbors were rejoicing over the fact that Japan had just scored a goal to tie Colombia 1-1.

As I listened to their shouts, I remembered one of the parables of Christ. "Either what woman having ten pieces of silver, if she lose one piece, doth not light a candle, and sweep the house, and seek diligently till she find it? And when she hath found it, she calleth her friends and her neighbours together, saying, Rejoice with me; for I have found the piece which I had lost. Likewise, I say unto you, there is joy in the presence of the angels of God over one sinner that repenteth." (Luke 15:8-10)

Like the people in my neighborhood who rejoiced when Japan scored a goal, the neighbors rejoiced with the woman who found the lost piece of silver. Jesus went on to say that the same thing happens when even one person repents of his sins and believes in Christ. The repentance of that sinner causes the angels in heaven to shout for joy.

Because we know this, the goal of our church ought to be a church that is constantly causing the angels in heaven to shout for joy through our zealous evangelism.

Unfortunately, the goal that Japan scored did not result in a victory, but the church that makes the angels in heaven shout for joy will be greatly blessed by the Lord.

"SOMETHING STINKS"

———— ❧ ————

The minute everyone entered the door of the church, they made an awful face. Some people even held their nose and said, "What's that awful smell?" The lobby was filled with the odor of rotten garbage. I had forgotten to take a bag of garbage home with me, so it had remained in the hot church for three days. I grabbed the bag and took it outside as quickly as possible, but the smell remained.

And then, when we entered the auditorium, the smell was just as bad. One of the ladies found some rotten food in a drawer and threw it away right away, but the smell remained. It was a very hot Sunday, so the smell of the rotten garbage was so strong we had to turn off the air conditioners and open all the windows.

According to First Samuel 16:7, "The Lord seeth not as man seeth; for man looketh on the outward appearance, but the Lord looketh on the heart." I wonder if the Lord ever says "something stinks" when He looks inside our heart and sees the garbage that is there.

What kind of garbage? "Out of the heart of men, proceed evil thoughts, adulteries, fornications, murders, thefts, covetousness, wickedness, deceit, lasciviousness, an evil eye, blasphemy, pride, foolishness:" (Mark 7:21-22)

When God looks inside our heart and says, "Something stinks," what should we do? "Let all bitterness, and wrath, and anger, and clamour, and evil speaking, be put away from you, with all malice." (Ephesians 4:31) "Put it away" – cast it out of your heart. And then, pray this prayer: "Create in me a clean heart, O God." (Psalm 51:10)

SONG OF VICTORY

The instant I entered the store, my face changed to a smile of joy because the music of one of my favorite songs was being played in the store. It was this song: (the Softbank Hawks Fight Song) ♪ Iza yuke muteki no wakataka gundan Iza yuke honoo no wakataka gundan. Warera no, warera no Softbank Hawks ♫

Again this year the Softbank Hawks won the Japan Series and became the champions of Japan. However, during the season the possibility of the Hawks winning the championship was remote. At one time, the Hawks fell to fifth place. They were 12 games behind first-place Seibu. However, the Hawks climbed to second place, defeated Seibu in the playoffs and then defeated Hiroshima in the Japan Series, so when I go shopping, I enjoy singing the Hawks' song of victory.

Sometimes Christians who are trying to obey the Word of God resemble this year's Hawks. We experience various trials. Our daily Christian life is an intense battle with our lusts. Now and then we give in to temptation. We listen to the voice of Satan and become discouraged.

However, according to Revelation, in the end, like the Hawks, we shall gain the victory. We shall gather around the throne of God with all Christians and sing this song of victory: "Blessing, and honour, and glory, and power, be unto him that sitteth upon the throne, and unto the Lamb for ever and ever." (Revelation 5:13)

Because we know the time will come when we shall sing the song of victory, let us be "steadfast, unmoveable, always abounding in the work of the Lord." (First Corinthians 15:58)

SOUR CHRISTIANS

———— ❧ ————

There is a *hassaku* tree in my backyard. (A *hassaku* is a hybrid of several citrus fruits. It resembles a grapefruit, but it is not as sour as a grapefruit.)

Hassaku ripen in the first part of February. This month (January), there was a strong wind one day and several of the *hassaku* fell to the ground. I picked them up, brought them into the house, washed them and tried to eat them. Because they were not fully ripened yet, they were more sour than usual.

There are Christians who resemble those *hassaku*. Because they are spiritually immature, they are sour. There were Christians like that in the church in Corinth. In First Corinthians 3:1 Paul called them "babes."

There are three characteristics of sour Christians. The first one is envy. "For ye are yet carnal: for whereas there is among you envying, and strife, and divisions, are ye not carnal, and walk as men?" (First Corinthians 3:3) The envy of a "sour" Christian causes strife in the church.

The second one is immorality. "It is reported commonly that there is fornication among you." (First Corinthians 5:1)

The third one is divisions. "I hear that there be divisions among you." (First Corinthians 11:18)

Envy, immorality, and divisions – these are the characteristics of a "sour" Christian who is spiritually immature. Let's search our hearts and make certain we have none of these characteristics lest we become a "sour" Christian who interferes with the unity of our church.

SOY, SEAFOOD, AND SALT

Yukio Yamori is an emeritus professor of Kyoto University. Also, he is the director of Mukogawa Women's University Institute for World Health Development. He spent twenty years doing research on longevity in twenty-five countries.

This is the conclusion of his research: "The important foods for health are the three S's – soy, seafood, and salt. We should be eating more food made from soy beans, more food taken from the sea, and we should decrease our intake of salt."

Certainly, eating too much salt is not good for our health. Lately my doctor has been saying this to me over and over again, so now I have to eat my salad without any salt. However, Christians should increase their salt. In Matthew 5:13 Christ said to His disciples, "Ye are the salt of the earth: but if the salt have lost his savour, wherewith shall it be salted? it is thenceforth good for nothing, but to be cast out, and to be trodden under foot of men."

As the salt of the earth, the disciples of Christ have two important roles. In the days when there were no refrigerators, salt was recognized as the best preservative. Likewise, by living as righteous a life as possible, Christians can help prevent the corruption of society.

Another important purpose of salt is to add flavor to food. Likewise, the role of Christians is to add flavor to the Christian life. Through a lifestyle that is overflowing with peace and joy, we can create in people a desire to try the Christian life. "Let your speech be always with grace, seasoned with salt." (Colossians 4:6)

STAIRS! I HATE STAIRS!

During November and December, we distribute a lot of flyers advertising our special evangelistic services, our children's services, our English Class services and our Christmas services. Two or three times I have distributed flyers in an area called Yayoigaoka, but I do not want to distribute flyers there again because there are too many stairs.

I have neuropathy in both feet, so I hate stairs. If I can reach the mailbox from the third step, I will climb the stairs, but when I cannot, I skip that house. If I climb a lot of stairs, after about thirty minutes, my feet will hurt so badly that I have to quit. In order to distribute as many flyers as possible, I have to avoid stairs. When I distribute flyers, I like to take Brother Nozomu with me. He is young, so I ask him to take care of the houses that have a lot of stairs.

In chapters 21 and 22 of Revelation there is a detailed description of heaven. We read about walls, gates, foundations and streets, but the word "stairs" does not appear even one time. (I do not know where the person who wrote "I'm Gonna Walk Dem Golden Stairs" got his idea from.) Maybe there are no stairs in heaven.

However, even if there are stairs in heaven, they will not be a problem for me because in heaven my body will be a body with no disabilities. Christians with physical disabilities and mental disabilities are looking forward to that time.

"For our conversation is in heaven; from whence also we look for the Saviour, the Lord Jesus who shall change our vile body, that it may be fashioned like unto his glorious body." (Philippians 3:20-21)

STAY AWAY!

Most people think there are only two species of poisonous snakes in Japan – the *habu* and the *mamushi*. Actually, there is one more – the *yamakagashi*. There are many *yamakagashi* in Honshu, Shikoku, and Kyushu. They are often spotted near lakes, rice paddies, and rivers. It is very difficult to tell if a snake is a *yamakagashi* or not, so the safest thing to do is to stay away from all snakes.

This is good advice for Christians too. In the Bible it is written, "Abstain from all appearance of evil." (First Thessalonians 5:22) Also, First Peter 2:11 teaches us to "abstain from fleshly lusts, which war against the soul."

If you knew there was a *yamakagashi* in a certain place, would you go near that place? A person who considers his life to be important would stay away from that place. Likewise, a Christian who wants to live a life that is pleasing to the Lord will stay away from places where he knows there are sins that will tempt him.

Also, a Christian who wants to live a life that will bring glory to God will stay away from people who tempt him to do things that are not right in the eyes of God. Proverbs 22:5 states, "Thorns and snares are in the way of the froward: he that doth keep his soul shall be far from them."

Verses ten and fifteen of chapter one of Proverbs warn us. "If sinners entice thee, consent thou not. My son, walk not thou in the way with them; refrain thy foot from their path."

Places and people who try to persuade us to participate in their sinful actions should be considered as dangerous as a *yamakagashi*.

STEPHANIE'S REVENGE

A missionary family who had just arrived in Japan stayed with us while they were looking for a house. The daughter, Stephanie, would usually sit next to me at the table. One night, when she was looking the other way, I took the bottle of mayonnaise and squirted some on her arm. Of course, she was shocked. During the time they stayed with us, I squirted mayonnaise or ketchup or mustard on her arm several times.

They served in Japan for several years but had to return to the States because of the illness of their son. More than twenty years passed. One year, while we were on furlough, we went to visit them. By this time, Stephanie was married and had a family of her own. One night during dinner when I was talking with her parents, suddenly I felt something cold on my arm. I looked and saw a big glob of mayonnaise. Holding a bottle of mayonnaise, Stephanie stood there with a big smile on her face.

The natural tendency of man is to seek revenge on others who have wronged us with their deeds or words. However, Christ taught a higher standard of living. In Luke 6:28 He said, "Bless them that curse you, and pray for them which despitefully use you."

Not only should we not take revenge on others, we should avoid actions and words that cause others to desire revenge against us. "See that none render evil for evil unto any man; but ever follow that which is good, both among yourselves, and to all men." (First Thessalonians 5:15)

Whether it is a harmless prank such as quirting mayonnaise on someone's arm or something much more serious, let's be careful of actions or words that may cause others to harbor bitterness against us.

SUDDENLY!

Do you remember where you were on March 11, 2011? I was in a hospital waiting room. <u>Suddenly,</u> a nurse ran in and turned on the television. Along with several other patients, I stood there with my mouth open and watched a massive tidal wave destroy a town. I remember the awfulness of that moment to this day.

Last week the History Channel broadcast a special program in memory of that disaster. The content was actual videos taken by witnesses of natural disasters around the world that happened <u>suddenly</u>. A lightning strike in Australia. Hailstorms, tornados, and floods in North America. A landslide in Brazil. An avalanche in Nepal. I sat there dumbfounded as I watched the videos of these events that had taken place <u>suddenly.</u>

The word "suddenly" appears in the Bible forty-one times. Two of those passages are especially impressionable. "For man also knoweth not his time: as the fishes that are taken in an evil net, and as the birds that are caught in the snare; so are the sons of men snared in an evil time, when it falleth <u>suddenly</u> upon them." (Ecclesiastes 9:12)

According to Proverbs 6:12-15, the calamity of a wicked man shall "come <u>suddenly</u>; <u>suddenly</u> shall he be broken without remedy." (Proverbs 6:12-15)

I am not advocating that we live in constant fear of a sudden disaster. What I am urging is for us to consider if we are ready to meet God if a natural disaster were to occur <u>suddenly</u> in the town where we live. "Boast not thyself of tomorrow; for thou knowest not what a day may bring forth." (Proverbs 27:1)

SWEETER AND SWEETER

Two doors down from the church there is a soba shop. (*Soba* is noodles made from buckwheat.) The wife of the owner of the shop comes to my Friday morning English class. I often go there for lunch between my morning class and afternoon class.

I have eaten several different kinds of soba there and they were all good, but it was the soup in which the soba is made that aroused my interest. After the meal, the owner brough me a small cup of it and said, "Drink this." Of course, the soba taste was strong. Then the owner added some onions and had me drink it. The taste was somewhat better.

Next, he added some soy sauce and had me drink it. It was much more delicious. Finally, he added some sort of stock and had me drink it one more time. It was even more delicious.

The soba soup which became more delicious and more delicious reminded me of the Christian's relationship with Christ. "O taste and see that the Lord is good: blessed is the man that trusteth in him." (Psalm 34:8)

I first tasted the goodness of Christ in 1955 and have been tasting His goodness for 56 years. Like the taste of the soba soup that became more and more delicious, the taste of the goodness of the Lord has become, as the song says, sweeter and sweeter.

"It gets <u>sweeter</u> as the days go by It gets <u>sweeter</u> as the <u>moments</u> fly

His love is richer, deeper, fuller, sweeter Sweeter, sweeter, <u>sweeter</u> as the days go by."

TASTELESS COFFEE

On Wednesday evening, while I am waiting for everyone to come to the Bible study, I fix some coffee. I put water, a filter, and some coffee into the pot and turn on the switch. After everyone has gathered, I announce, "The coffee is ready."

Two or three weeks ago when I did that, two of the ladies went to fix coffee for everyone. Suddenly I heard them laughing. Thinking, "What is so funny?" I went to see. When they poured coffee into the cups, only hot water came out because although I had put in water and a filter, I had forgotten to put in the coffee.

Coffee with no coffee in it is tasteless coffee. Likewise, a Christian life without the Word of God is a tasteless life, for it is the Bible that adds flavor to the life of the Christian. According to Psalm 19:10, the words of the Bible are sweeter also than honey and the honeycomb. In Psalm 119:103 David wrote, "How sweet are thy words unto my taste! yea, sweeter than honey to my mouth!"

If, at the present time, your Christian life is a life with very little delight and joy, try doing what Jeremiah did. "Thy words were found, and I did eat them; and thy word was unto me the joy and rejoicing of mine heart." (Jeremiah 15:16)

Every morning when you eat breakfast, open the Bible and taste it with your eyes. If you will do so, your life that is now like tasteless coffee will become a life of delight and joy.

"The statutes of the LORD are right, rejoicing the heart." (Psalm 19:8)

THE AMERICAN DREAM

Have you ever heard the Expression "The American Dream?" This expression manifests the desire of every American. 1-Individual freedom. 2-Success in work. 3-A happy life. 4-Your own home. The person who accomplishes these four things is said to be "living the dream." By the time my wife and I could "live the dream," I was already 56 years old.

Until recently all Japanese desired the same four things. I suppose we could call it "The Japanese Dream." Japanese especially want to own their own home. However, according to a poll conducted by the Japanese government, now only 79.8% want to buy their own home. This is the first time this number has fallen below 80% in twelve years. 12.5% of the remaining 21.2% are satisfied with living in a rented home.

Because land is so expensive in Japan, many of the 79.8% who want to own their own home are unable to accomplish "The Japanese Dream." However, even if they are not able to own their own home on this earth, people who believe in Jesus Christ need not give up on the dream of living in your own home. In John 14:1-3 Jesus made this promise. "Let not your heart be troubled: ye believe in God, believe also in me. In my Father's house are many mansions: if it were not so, I would have told you. I go to prepare a place for you. And if I go and prepare a place for you, I will come again, and receive you unto myself; that where I am, there ye may be also."

Jesus is preparing a place for us in heaven, so if you live in an apartment or rented home, rejoice. Some day you will live in the home that God Himself has prepared for you. It is no more dream or hope. It is a fact based on the promise of Christ.

THE BALL IN THE OCEAN

———— ❧ ————

One day when our church had lunch on the beach, I went for a walk and saw a ball in the ocean. The water was not very deep where the ball was, so I waded into the ocean and picked up the ball. I took it home and placed it near my desk.

Every time I look at that ball, I think about various things. For example, whose ball was it? Maybe it belonged to a child. What were the circumstances when the ball went into the ocean? When the ball flew to a place where it could not be retrieved, did the child cry?

Also, I think about the fact that the ball is no longer able to fulfill its purpose. Maybe the ball was made to bring joy to a child or to be used in a baseball game for young men. However, the instant the ball went into the ocean, it became something that was no longer able to fulfill its purpose.

Another thing that I think about is how much that ball resembles man. According to the Bible, man was created to give glory to God. In Isaiah 43:7 God said, "Even every one that is called by my name: for I have created him for my glory, I have formed him; yea, I have made him." Also, according to Revelation 4:11, man was created to give pleasure to God. "Thou art worthy, O Lord, to receive glory and honour and power: for thou hast created all things, and for thy pleasure they are and were created."

What about our life? Does our life give glory to God? Does our life bring pleasure to God? If not, we are like the ball I found in the ocean. Our life is a life that has lost its purpose.

THE BEAUTIFUL NECKTIE
I DID NOT WANT

The members of my Friday English class gave me a birthday present. It was a beautiful necktie. When I saw the necktie, I was very happy, but at the same time, I was troubled because I cannot tie neckties skillfully. Since I was young, I have used only clip-on ties, so it has been many years since I tied a necktie.

It was a beautiful necktie, and to me it showed the friendship of my students, so I decided to wear it to the next English class. Before going to the class, I tried tying the tie skillfully several times, but I just could not get it right. The last time I tried to tie it, the bottom part ended up longer than the top part. It was time to leave for the class, so I left the tie like that and covered it up with my coat. After the class, I opened my coat and showed them the tie, and they all laughed.

Imagine the image of me hiding my tie with my coat. That is the image of man who has been trying to hide his sins from God since the beginning of the world. According to Genesis 3:7-8, when Adam and Eve sinned against God, they tried to hide their sin.

Mankind still has not changed. To this day we make an effort to hide our sins from God; however, no matter how hard we try, we cannot hide our sins from Him, for in First Samuel 16:7 it is written, "Man looketh on the outward appearance, but the Lord looketh on the heart."

In Psalm 44:21 it is written, "He knoweth the secrets of the heart." We must not try to play hide-and-seek with God, for in Proverbs 28:13 it is written, "He that covereth his sins shall not prosper: but whoso confesseth and forsaketh them shall have mercy."

THE BIG SPOON AND
THE LITTLE SPOON

When I ate lunch with everyone at the Kitakyushu church, the ladies of the church said, "Pastor Board, please sit here." There were several seats still empty, so I thought, "Why do I have to sit here?"

As soon as I sat down, I notice a big spoon, the size of a serving spoon, by my plate. I picked it up and asked, "What is this?" When I did, the ladies all burst into laughter. I pretended to be angry and said, "What are you laughing at?"

They said, "Pastor Board, give us that spoon. We will bring you a different one." This time they brought me a little spoon, the size used to feed babies. Again, they laughed and I pretended to be angry. I am always playing jokes on them, but this time the joke was on me.

Later, when I thought about the big spoon and the little spoon the ladies had used to play a joke on me, the image of the blessings of the Lord and our offerings to Him came to my mind.

Just as we are exhorted to do in First Corinthians 16:2, on the first day of the week, with joy we give our offerings to the Lord as He has prospered us. Second Corinthians 9:7 states that the Lord loves it when we do that. Furthermore, according to Malachi 3:10, the Lord will open the windows of heaven and pour out a blessing on us.

We take a spoon like a baby spoon and offer to the Lord, but the Lord takes a spoon like a serving spoon and blesses us. "God is able to make all grace abound toward you; that ye, always having all sufficiency in all things, may abound to every good work." (Second Corinthians 9:8)

THE BOTTOMLESS JAR

In America, there are several kinds of pickles that cannot be bought in Japan. One of these is "Bread and Butter Pickles." During the Great Depression of the 1930's, many Americans ate these pickles with bread and butter, so the name "Bread and Butter Pickles" was given to this kind of pickle.

I love Bread and Butter Pickles, especially on sandwiches. Recently, when my missionary friend, Cristy Wyatt, made some of these pickles, she gave me a jar of them. She told me, "This jar is a bottomless jar. When the pickles are all gone, I will fill the jar again." Now I am enjoying a few pickles from the bottomless jar almost every day.

The bottomless jar of pickles is similar to the love of God. If we put the love of God in a jar, we would see that it is a bottomless jar. The love of God is an eternal love that has no end. According to Jeremiah 31:3, God loves us with an everlasting love.

John 3:16 teaches us that the love of God is an impartial love. "For God so loved the world, that he gave his only begotten Son, that whosoever believeth in him should not perish, but have everlasting life."

Also, His love for us is an inseparable love. "Neither death, nor life, nor angels, nor principalities, nor powers, nor things present, nor things to come, Nor height, nor depth, nor any other creature, shall be able to separate us from the love of God, which is in Christ Jesus our Lord." (Romans 8:38-39)

Eternal, impartial, inseparable – yes, the jar of God's love is a bottomless jar.

THE BROKEN WALL

In 2009 a breakwater was completed at the mouth of Kamaishi Bay in Iwate Prefecture. It was 20 meters thick and 2 meters long. The size of the foundation of the breakwater was 7 million cubic meters. This is 63 times the size of Tokyo Dome. The depth of the breakwater was 63 meters, so it was recognized by the Guinness Book of Records as the deepest breakwater in the world.

The breakwater was built to withstand a magnitude 8.5 earthquake and tidal wave. When the magnitude 9.0 earthquake occurred on March 11, the breakwater was broken by a massive tidal wave. According to the calculations of a Waseda University ocean engineer, the momentum of the tidal wave that broke the breakwater was the momentum of 250 jumbo jets flying at 1000 kilometers an hour.

Certainly the breakwater in Kamaishi Bay was a huge wall, but there was another wall that was much deeper, much longer, much bigger and much thicker. It was the wall of sin between God and man. When man rebelled against the commandment of God and sinned, a wall was formed between the holy God and sinful man.

Because of this wall, we became people who have no hope, cannot approach God, have enmity against God and have no peace. However, there was something deeper, bigger, longer and thicker than this wall. It was the love of God. His love sent us a Savior to break down the wall of sin that separates us from Him. "Now in Christ Jesus ye who sometimes were far off are made nigh by the blood of Christ. For he is our peace, who hath made both one, and hath broken down the middle wall of partition between us." (Ephesians 2:13-14)

THE CHERRY BLOSSOM
TREES ARE BACK

The cherry blossom trees had gotten so big that they formed a canopy over the road. Many people came to Takamidai just to drive through the tunnel of flowers.

However, the roots of the trees became a danger to the people living in Takamidai. More and more people were hurt when they tripped over the roots growing through the sidewalk, so several years ago the city removed all the trees and planted new ones. Takamidai seemed like a lonely place without the trees. However, the trees are back. They are growing larger and larger, so everyone is enjoying the beauty of the cherry blossoms once again.

Although the blossoms are beautiful, there is one regretful fact. They only bloom for a week or ten days at the most and then they fall to the wayside. If there is a heavy rain or strong wind, the blossoms may last for only three or four days.

The Bible compares the life of man to a flower like the cherry blossom. "For all flesh is as grass, and all the glory of man as the flower of grass. The grass withereth, and the flower thereof falleth away." (First Peter 1:24)

Someday, we too will fall like the cherry blossom, but First Peter 1:3 declares that God has "begotten us again unto a lively hope by the resurrection of Jesus Christ from the dead." Christians do not fear death. Our hope is based on the promise of Christ. "I am the resurrection, and the life: he that believeth in me, though he were dead, yet shall he live." (John 11:25)

THE CHRISTIAN'S RIVAL

On July 2nd, the Japan National Student Association conducted its 49th Intercollegiate English Oratorical Contest. The winner was Miss Kanako Bizen of Sophia University. The title of her speech was "Win Against the Rival."

Miss Bizen said, "Talking of a rival, we usually come up with a person who competes in the same contest, competing with us. However, my rival right now is not another contestant in front of me. My rival is myself."

It is the same with Christians. If the question were asked, "Who is the rival of the Christian?" many people would reply, "The devil." Certainly, the devil is our greatest enemy, but the rival of the Christian who is daily trying to live a life that is pleasing to the Lord is himself.

The Apostle Paul knew that his rival was himself. In First Corinthians 9:27 he wrote, "But I keep under my body, and bring it into subjection: lest that by any means, when I have preached to others, I myself should be a castaway."

Every Christian is fighting the same battle daily. It is a battle with self that does not want to read the Bible, with self that does not want to pray, with self that does not want to evangelize and with self that does not want to attend the church services faithfully. Our battle with the devil begins with the fight with ourself.

"If any man will come after me, let him deny himself, and take up his cross, and follow me." (Matthew 16:24)

THE CHRISTIAN'S SEAT BELT

When you go out, do you put your child in a child seat and lock the seat belt? Please do so. According to data of the Japan Police Agency, the traffic accident fatality rate for children who are not using a child seat is 13.4 times higher than children who use a child seat. The law says that all children six years old and under must sit in a child seat. However, 29.5% of the parents of Japan do not obey this law. If you have small children, please join the 70.5% of the parents who obey this law.

There is a seat belt for all Christians too. (Of course, the word "seat belt" is not found in the Bible. The Bible uses the word "girdle.") In Ephesians 6:11 we are commanded to put on the whole armor of God, that we may be able to stand against the wiles of the devil. One piece of armor that every Christian should put on is the girdle of truth. "Stand therefore, having your loins girt about with truth." (Ephesians 6:14)

The devil is the crafty enemy of every Christian, so it is extremely important that we put on the girdle of truth lest we be deceived by his schemes. In First Timothy 4:1 it is written, "Now the Spirit speaketh expressly, that in the latter times some shall depart from the faith, giving heed to seducing spirits, and doctrines of devils."

To avoid becoming a Christian who gives heed to these deceiving spirits, let us firmly fasten on the girdle of truth. What truth? According to John 17:17, the words of God written in the Bible are the truth that we should fasten around us.

Every day when we go out, before we fasten the seat belt of our car, let us fasten the girdle of truth around us by reading the Bible.

THE CONCERT MASTER

I am seventy-two years old but have never been to a symphony concert. However, one of the ladies of the Kokura church is a member of the Kitakyushu Symphony Orchestra, so several members of the church and I went to a concert performed by the Orchestra. I rejoiced to hear the compositions of Strauss and Haydin and Beethoven live for the first time. I especially enjoyed the performance of a trumpet player from France.

I was told that the first violinist is referred to as the "concert master." After all the members of the orchestra had entered, she entered. I was especially interested by what happened next. She played a note on her violin and all the members of the orchestra tuned their instruments to her violin.

In many ways, a church resembles an orchestra. When all the members join their talents to one another, we can build a church that is pleasing to the Lord. However, similar to an orchestra, there must be a concert master.

Who should be the concert master of the church. The pastor? The most zealous member? The most talented member? According to Ephesians 4:15-16, the concert master of the church is Christ. "But speaking the truth in love, may grow up into him in all things, which is the head, even <u>Christ</u>: <u>From whom</u> the whole body fitly joined together and compacted by that which every joint supplieth, according to the effectual working in the measure of every part, maketh increase of the body unto the edifying of itself in love."

The growing church is the church that has Christ as its concert master.

THE COURAGE OF A
SIX-YEAR-OLD GIRL

My son and his family live in the city of Kirishima in Kagoshima Prefecture. He has two children, a 6-year-old girl named Nina and a 3-year-old boy named Noah. Nina is in the first grade at a Japanese school.

The other day the teacher took Nina and her classmates to a shrine. Thankfully, the teacher did not make the students worship the god of the shrine. There was a special rock at that shrine. The teacher pointed at the rock and said, "This rock is a god." The other students said nothing, but my granddaughter spoke up in front of the teacher and the other students and said, "That rock is not a real god."

I wonder if we who are already adults and young people would have the courage to refuse to worship false gods. In the Famous Ten Commandments it is written clearly, "Thou shalt not make unto thee any graven image, or any likeness of anything that is in heaven above, or that is in the earth beneath, or that is in the water under the earth. Thou shalt not bow down thyself to them, nor serve them." (Exodus 20:4-5)

Also, in First Corinthians 10:14 it is written, "Flee from idolatry," and in First John 5:21 the Bible says, "Keep yourselves from idols." Furthermore, chapter 1 of Romans teaches us that idols are the creation of foolish people with dark hearts who had become vain in their imaginations. (1:21-23 and 25)

After we become Christians, we should never worship anything other than the true and living God. When we are urged by our family and friends to worship something or someone other than the true God, let us have the same courage that was in my six-year-old granddaughter and answer clearly, "I cannot do that. That is not the true God."

THE DETOURS OF LIFE

Last Sunday I preached at the Sasebo Baptist Church. I had to leave at 7:30 to be there in time to teach Sunday School. If I take the Kyushu Expressway and then the Nagasaki Expressway, I can drive there in a little over two hours.

However, there had been heavy rain that morning, so the Kyushu Expressway was closed. I had to take a detour on the regular roads, so I did not make it in time for Sunday School. After the morning service, I left without eating lunch, hoping the expressway would be open by now, but to my dismay, now the Nagasaki Expressway was closed too. The trip home took four and one-half hours.

Weather-related conditions that interfere with our travel plans are troublesome. However, events that interfere with the plans of our life are even worse. When, for some unforeseen event, our life has to take a detour, let us remember three things.

First, if the cause of the detour is our own disobedience to the will of God, let's go back to the place where we left the path of God and start from there.

Second, when the detours of life occur according to the will of God, let's trust in the plan of God. When the life of Job became a detour because of many calamities, he wrote, "Thought he slay me, yet will I trust him." (Job 13:15)

Third, even when our life takes a detour, remember, "The Lord thy God is with thee whithersoever thou goest." (Joshua 1:9)

THE DRUNKEN FLOWER

During my Friday English class, I give the students an opportunity to talk about any subject. One student likes to talk about the flowers he is growing in his garden. One day he brought a strange flower called *suifuyou*. The color of the flower is white in the morning, but as the sun shines on it, the color changes. In the afternoon, it is a pretty pink color. By dusk, the color of the flower is the red color of the face of a person who has become drunk with wine, so it is called "the drunken flower."

This flower resembles the human heart. According to the Bible, all people are born sinners. "Among whom also we all had our conversation in times past in the lusts of our flesh, fulfilling the desires of the flesh and of the mind; and <u>were by nature the children of wrath</u>, even as others." (Ephesians 2:3)

What is the color of the human heart at the time of birth? Many people think it is black; however, according to Isaiah 1:18, it is red. Red is a color that is hard to remove. For example, it is difficult to remove a red stain on clothing. There is only one thing that can remove the red color of sin from the human heart. That one thing is the pure blood that flowed from the body of Christ as He hung on the cross dying for our sins. "The blood of Jesus Christ his Son cleanseth us from all sin." (First John 1:7) According to Revelation 1:5, Christ has "washed us from our sins in his own blood."

The "drunken flower" is white in the morning and red in the evening. The heart of the person who believes in Christ is the opposite. The human heart is red at first but becomes white when a person repents of his sins and receives Christ as his Savior.

KEN BOARD

THE EMPTY WAITING ROOM

I have lived in Japan for 41 years, but the other day I saw something I had never seen before. It was an empty waiting room at the clinic where I go. There is no appointment system in Japan, so when you go to the hospital or a clinic, the possibility is strong that you will have to wait a long time. This is a problem for me because I become irritated when I am made to wait very long.

However, when I walked into the clinic recently, I was surprised. There was no one in the waiting room. I was called into the exam room almost immediately. I said to him, "What happened?" He was puzzled by my question, so I explained, "Today there was no one in the waiting room. Have you already healed everyone in Kitakyushu City.?" He laughed.

There will never come a time when everyone has been healed, so the work of a doctor is a work that never ends. The same can be said of the work of the church. In Mark 16:15 Jesus said, "Go ye into all the world and preach the gospel to every creature."

The words "to every creature" make clear the mission of the church. As long as there is one person who has not heard the gospel, we must continue to evangelize. Through regular church services, special services, tract and flyer distribution, and Sunday School we are trying to reach everyone in this area with the gospel. In spite of this, there are still many people who have never heard the gospel, so let's be diligent in evangelism, zealous in our service and faithful in our giving.

The disciples in Ephesus are our example. "All they which dwelt in Asia heard the word of the Lord Jesus." (Acts 19:10)

THE ETERNAL FLAME WENT OUT!

Have you heard? The 1964 Tokyo Olympic flame went out four years ago. When the 2020 Olympics were awarded to Tokyo, the media became interested in the 1964 Olympic flame that was housed in a sports facility in Kagoshima Prefecture. However, when they asked about the flame, an official admitted that the flame had gone out on November 21, 2013. The Olympic flame is called the "Eternal Flame," but it died out.

However, according to the Bible, there are things that shall never die out.

The existence of the true God is an existence that shall never die out. "Before the mountains were brought forth, or ever thou hadst formed the earth and the world, even from everlasting to everlasting, thou art God." (Psalm 90:2)

The mercy of God toward us is an eternal mercy that shall never die out. "The mercy of the Lord is from everlasting to everlasting upon them that fear him." (Psalm 103:17)

The salvation that God gives to the person who believes in the Savior Jesus Christ is an eternal salvation that shall never die out. "The gift of God is eternal life through Jesus Christ our Lord." (Romans 6:23)

The Word of God is an eternal Word that shall never die out. In Matthew 24:35 Christ said, "Heaven and earth shall pass away, but my words shall not pass away."

Everything in this world is a fleeting thing like the Olympic flame. Let's put our hope in the eternal mercy and the eternal salvation and the eternal Word of the eternal God.

THE FENCE OF LIFE

When I went to Okinawa last month, Pastor Saitoh of the Okinawa Bible Baptist Church and I went swimming in the East China Sea. I have seen the movie "Jaws," so when we first went into the water, I was a little bit nervous. I asked Pastor Saitoh, "Do sharks ever come here?" Laughing, he replied, "Look out there. There is a fence, so the sharks cannot come in here."

Later, two young men who were swimming near the fence were warned by the lifeguard. "Do not touch the fence. If you break the fence, the *habu* (a poisonous snake) will come in here." A fence was necessary to protect the swimmers from sharks and snakes.

In the same way, our soul needs a fence to protect it. That fence is the Word of God. In what way does the Word of God protect us? It protects us from sin. "Your word I have hidden in my heart, that I might not sin against you." (Psalm 119:11)

It protects us from straying from the right path. "Your word is a lamp to my feet and a light to my path." (Psalm 119:105)

It protects us from the wiles of the devil. "Put on the whole armor of God, that you may be able to stand against the wiles of the devil. Take the helmet of salvation, and the sword of the Spirit, which is the word of God." (Ephesians 6:11,17)

Different from the fence that protected people from sharks and poisonous snakes, the Word of God that protects us from sin, straying, and the wiles of the devil cannot be broken, so we can swim safely in the sea of life.

THE FORBIDDEN LETTER

On October thirty-first, a dinner was held at the Akasaka Imperial Garden. A politician opposed to nuclear weapons handed a letter to the Emperor. Handing a letter directly to the Emperor is forbidden, so he is under heavy criticism from members of his own party and opposition parties. "A shameful act," "disrespectful behavior," they are saying. As a result, he will no longer be invited to parties where the Emperor attends.

Approaching people like emperors, kings, presidents and prime ministers is not permitted. I am a tax-paying American citizen, but if I call the White House and ask to speak directly to the President, it will not be allowed.

However, amazingly, according to the Bible, we can speak directly to the God who created the heaven and the earth. There are many people who believe that, when we talk to God, we must talk to Him through a priest or Mary or a pastor. However, according to the Bible, God will hear the prayers of people who speak to Him directly. In Psalm 4:3 David wrote, "The Lord will hear when I call unto him."

Furthermore, the Bible teaches that we can speak to God anytime, anywhere. Some people, to have God listen to their prayer, will go to a church or a temple or a shrine and give offerings. But, according to Second Chronicles 7:14, if we will humble ourselves, seek the face of God and turned from our wicked ways, God will hear us.

Anywhere. Anytime. Anybody. Freely. "Let us therefore come boldly unto the throne of grace, that we may obtain mercy, and find grace to help in time of need." (Hebrews 4:16)

THE FOREVER LAMP

When I was shaving, the bathroom light suddenly went out. I removed the light bulb and put in a new one. As I carried the old bulb to the trashcan, I noticed these words written on the bulb. [Forever Lamp] When I saw those words, I could not help but laugh, because when I moved to this house four and a half years ago, the owner put new light bulbs in the bathroom. The light bulb that was supposed to shine forever lasted just four and a half years.

As I looked at the Forever Lamp in my hand, I thought, "this light bulb that burned out in just four and a half years is a symbol of the things of this world." According to the Bible, this world and everything in it are temporary things like a burnt-out light bulb. "The world passeth away." (First John 2:17) "The fashion of this world passeth away." (First Corinthians 7:31)

Every valuable thing that we make important is nothing more than a temporary thing, so we should focus our hearts on the truth written in Second Corinthians 4:18. "While we look not at the things which are seen, but at the things which are not seen: for the things which are seen are temporal; but the things which are not seen are eternal."

The burnt-out Forever Lamp proves the words of Christ written in Matthew 6:19-20. "Lay not up for yourselves treasures upon earth, where moth and rust doth corrupt, and where thieves break through and steal. But lay up for yourselves treasures in heaven, where neither moth nor rust doth corrupt, and where thieves do not break through nor steal."

Stop and take a look around your house. Nothing that you see is forever,

THE FOUR-YEAR-OLD GRANDFATHER

———— ❧ ————

When I went to Okinawa the other day, a funny thing happened. When I checked in at the counter, the girl who put my name into the computer had a startled face. She said, "According to the computer, you are four years old." Laughing, I replied, "I want to be younger, but I do not want to be four years old."

After hearing my true age, the girl changed the information in the computer and gave me my boarding pass. Still smiling as I walked toward the gate, I was thinking, "I, who am a 74-year-old grandfather with seven grandchildren, became four years old."

The Bible too speaks of people who, although they were up in years, were still like small children. In First Corinthians 3:1-2 Paul wrote this about the believers in Corinth: "I, brethren, could not speak unto you as unto spiritual, but as unto carnal, even as unto babes in Christ. I have fed you with milk, and not with meat: for hitherto ye were not able to bear it, neither yet now are ye able."

Paul wrote similar words in Hebrews 5:12. "For when for the time ye ought to be teachers, ye have need that one teach you again which be the first principles of the oracles of God; and are become such as have need of milk, and not of strong meat."

According to Ephesians 4:14, one of the characteristics of spiritually immature Christians is that they are "tossed to and fro and carried about with every wind of doctrine."

According to God's computer, how old are you?

THE GOD WHO CRIES

Lately events called *ruikatsu* are being held in Tokyo and other areas. About 40 people attend each of these events. First, they listen to some sad stories and then they watch a sad video. Next, they listen to a speech about the benefits of crying. Finally, the participants discuss the stories and videos that made them cry. This event lasts about ninety minutes and is free.

When I was in junior high school and high school, we called guys who cried a "crybaby" or a "sissy." We told them, "Real men don't cry." However, in the Bible, in Ecclesiastes 3:1 and 4 it is written, "To everything there is a season, a time for every purpose under heaven: A time to weep, and a time to laugh."

Amazingly, in the Bible we can see a God who cries. (Luke 19:41) "When he was come near, he beheld the city, and wept over it." Why did Christ weep over Jerusalem? "O Jerusalem, Jerusalem, thou that killest the prophets, and stonest them which are sent unto thee, how often would I have gathered thy children together, even as a hen gathereth her chickens under her wings, and ye would not!" (Matthew 23:37) His tears manifested His passionate concern for the salvation of His people.

Different from the "gods" made of wood or stone, the God of the Bible is a God who can weep. He is a God who can sympathize with us. (Hebrews 4:15)

Let us believe in the God who weeps for us. Let us love Him and follow Him. Also, just as Christ wept over the people of Jerusalem, let us weep for our family and friends who do not know Christ.

THE HALF-AND-HALF FLAG

Japan and the United States were to battle for the Women's World Cup Championship. This match produced mixed feelings in the hearts of Americans who had lived in Japan a long time. For example, as an American, I wanted the United States to win, but I wanted Japan to win too. No matter which team won, I could rejoice.

My daughter, Tabitha, who was born in Japan and lived there several years had the same feeling. On the day of the match, she posted a picture of a flag on Facebook. It was a half-and-half flag, Half of it was the American flag and the other half was the Japanese flag. That flag brilliantly expressed the feelings of Americans who love both America and Japan.

I suppose a half-and-half feeling is okay in sports, but it will not work in the matter of faith. Our faith must not be a half-and-half faith. According to First Kings, the people of Israel went away from God and began to worship Baal. One day, Elijah, the prophet of the Lord and the prophets of Baal gathered on Mount Carmel and held a showdown to determine the true God.

Before the showdown, Elijah said to the people of Israel, "How long halt ye between two opinions? if the LORD be God, follow him: but if Baal, then follow him." Joshua said the same thing in Joshua 24:15. "If it seem evil unto you to serve the LORD, choose you this day whom ye will serve; whether the gods which your fathers served that were on the other side of the flood, or the gods of the Amorites, in whose land ye dwell: but as for me and my house, we will serve the LORD." When it comes to the matter of faith, it has to be all or nothing.

THE HOLE IN THE BALLOON

When I went to a Hawks' baseball game with a friend from church, I took two balloons with me. (There is a custom to blow up balloons and release them in the middle of the seventh inning at all Hawks' games.) I had bought the balloons two years ago and kept them in a drawer to use the next time I went to a game.

In the top of the seventh inning, I gave one of the balloons to my friend. He tried and tried to blow it up but could not do it. He checked the balloon carefully and said to me, "There is a hole in this balloon." I apologized for giving him a balloon with a hole in it. When I tried to blow up my balloon, the results were the same. There was a hole in my balloon too.

A balloon with a hole in it is useless. There are other things that are of no use if they have a hole in them, for example, a cup or a bucket or a boat. There is one more – the Bible. If there was even one "hole" (one error or contradiction) in the Bible, we could not trust the entire Bible.

Our church believes that there is not one error or contradiction in the Bible. "The law of the Lord is perfect, converting the soul: the testimony of the Lord is sure, making wise the simple. The statutes of the Lord are right, rejoicing the heart: the commandment of the Lord is pure, enlightening the eyes." (Psalm 19:7-8)

A Bible with even one error in it is no different than a balloon with a hole in it. Therefore, God has given us a perfect Bible. "All scripture is given by inspiration of God, and is profitable for doctrine, for reproof, for correction, for instruction in righteousness." (Second Timothy 3:16)

THE LAST CRY OF A DYING ROOSTER

Peter denied the Lord three times and then the rooster crowed. When I preached on this passage, I thought of a way to make the sermon more dramatic. I found the sound of a rooster crowing on the Internet and recorded it on a small tape recorder. During my sermon I would say, "And then Peter heard this sound," and the audience would hear the rooster crowing. It would be a dramatic climax to my sermon.

However, when I put the tape recorder into my briefcase, unknowingly I moved the speed lever from normal to slow. Just like I planned, during the sermon I said, "And then Peter heard this sound," and I turned on the tape recorder. However, what the audience heard was not "Cock-a-doodle-doo" but "Cooooooooock-aaa-doooodle-doooo." It sounded like the last cry of a dying rooster. It was supposed to be the climax of my sermon, but everyone was roaring with laughter.

My plan to make the sermon more dramatic was an excellent plan. If it had gone smoothly, it would have been a wonderful sermon. However, because of one small mistake, my wonderful sermon was ruined.

Just as my carelessness interfered with my sermon, our act of disobedience on our part may interfere with the plan of God. For example, because of fear of the inhabitants of the land, the children of Israel disobeyed the voice of God and had to spend forty years wandering in the wilderness. (Numbers 14)

When God shows His plan to us, let us obey His voice without fear. "Be strong and of a good courage; be not afraid, neither be thou dismayed: for the Lord thy God is with thee whithersoever thou goest." (Joshua 1:9)

THE LETTER THAT ARRIVED
TEN YEARS LATER

On January 10, 2004, Chie Oshino, who was working as a bus guide in Aichi Prefecture, wrote a letter to her parents living in Otsuchi town in Iwate Prefecture. She left the letter in care of the Meiji-Mura Museum and asked that it be delivered 10 years later.

Later she moved back to Otsuchi and worked at the town office. She was working there on March 11, 2011 when the building was swept away by a tidal wave. She is still missing to this day.

Three years later, on January 12, 2014, the letter that she wrote 10 years earlier arrived at the home of her parents. The content of the letter was her work and marriage. These words were in the letter: "I owe a lot to you, dad and mom, so I will take care of the two of you from now on." How precious that letter must be to Mr. and Mrs. Oshino.

When I read the story of the letter of Miss Oshino, I remembered my own experience. In September of 2001 I went to preach at a church in Hokkaido. While I was there, my wife called and said, "Today your mother suddenly went home to be with the Lord." I wept because I did not have the opportunity to thank my mother before she went to heaven.

Just as it is written in the Bible, we do not know what will happen tomorrow, so today while we and our parents are still alive, let's thank them in some way.

"Hearken unto thy father that begat thee, and despise not thy mother when she is old." (Proverbs 23:22) "Thy father and thy mother shall be glad, and she that bare thee shall rejoice." (Proverbs 23: 25)

THE LOST SLIPPER

I have neuropathy, so I must wear slippers that I can adjust to my feet. If I wear regular slippers, my feet will hurt, so wherever I go, I take my slippers with me. When I went to Tokyo last month to preach at the Tokyo Bible Baptist Church, I took them with me.

The second day in Tokyo, Pastor Saitoh and his wife took me to the place where the Tokyo sumo tournaments are held, to a hot spring, and to a restaurant. When we returned home, I noticed that one of my slippers was missing. One of the slippers must have fallen out of the car somewhere.

It was evening already, so I went to my room. Although they were tired, Pastor Saitoh and his wife went to search for my lost slipper. They found it in the parking lot of Ryogoku Kokugikan. They returned it to me at breakfast the next morning. I was so happy!

There is a similar story in the Bible, a parable about a lost sheep. "What man of you, having an hundred sheep, if he lose one of them, doth not leave the ninety and nine in the wilderness, and go after that which is lost, until he find it? And when he hath found it, he layeth it on his shoulders, rejoicing."

According to Isaiah 53:6, that lost sheep represents every one of us. "All we like sheep have gone astray; we have turned every one to his own way." The shepherd who came searching for us is Jesus Christ. "For the Son of man is come to seek and to save that which was lost." (Luke 19:10)

The loving Savior wants to find you and bring you back home.

THE MARATHON THAT
LASTED 54 YEARS

The 1912 Olympics were held in Sweden at Stockholm. Only two Japanese participated in the games. One of them was Kanakuri Shinzou who was called "the father of the marathon" in Japan. He was born in the town of Tamana in Kumamoto Prefecture.

Weakened by the 18-day trip to Sweden, he fainted during the marathon. A farming family found him and helped him recover. Ashamed of his failure, he returned to Japan without telling anyone.

For 50 years the Sweden Olympic Committee thought he was missing, but in 1967 they discovered he was still alive and living in Japan, A Swedish TV company offered him the opportunity to return to Sweden and complete the marathon. He accepted the offer and returned to Sweden and finished the marathon, so it turned out to be a marathon that took 54 years, 8 months, 6 days, 5 hours and 32 minutes.

The Bible compares the Christian life to a marathon. "Let us lay aside every weight, and the sin which doth so easily beset us, and let us run with patience the race that is set before us," (Hebrews 12:1) There may be times when we too are weakened by trials and troubles and faint on our journey, However, after we recover, let's return to the marathon of our life and run all the way to the finish line.

The Apostle Paul left us a good example. Although he experienced many trials during his journey, he wrote these words in Second Timothy 4:8. "I have finished my course." God has given each one of us a course to run. Even if we faint now and then along the way, let's get up and keep running.

THE MISSING APPLES

The wife of Pastor Kirino called me. "Pastor Board, did the apples arrive?" I replied, "Apples? No." She said, "We sent you some apples. They should have arrived already." I told her, "Maybe they will come today. If they do not, I will call you tomorrow."

Right after that, I received a call from the store that had sent the apples. "Have the apples arrived?" "No, not yet." Three days later the daughter of Mrs. Kirino called me. "Pastor, did the apples arrive?" "No, not yet."

Suddenly I remembered two boxes that had arrived five days earlier. I had ordered several books from the Christian bookstore in Fukuoka, so I just assumed that both of the boxes contained books. I told Miss Kirino, "Wait just a minute," and went into the room where I had placed the boxes. There were books in the box on top, but the word "APPLES" was written in large letters on the other box. The apples that had been missing for five days were right in front of my eyes. The apples that the store and Mrs. Kirino and her daughter were searching for were right near me all that time.

My mistake reminded me of a mistake that many people make. They are searching for God, but God is right beside us. "That they should seek the Lord, if haply they might feel after him, and find him, though he be not far from every one of us:" (Acts 17:27) Many people go to shrines and temples searching for God, but the truth is that God is searching for us. "The Son of Man has come to seek and to save that which was lost." (Luke 19:10) It is said that "God is only a prayer away." Try it and see. You will discover that the words in Psalm 145:18 are true. "The Lord is nigh unto all them that call upon him, to all that call upon him in truth."

THE MISTAKE THAT RUINED MY SERMON

In my sermon, I told the story about a cowboy who rode into town every weekend, tied his horse in front of the saloon and went in and got drunk. One day the cowboy became a Christian. The next Sunday, he went into town, tied his horse in front of the saloon and went to church. When the pastor of the church saw this, he told the cowboy, "Now that you are a Christian, you should not tie your horse up in front of the saloon any longer." Of course, the point of the story was that, once you become a Christian, your conduct should change.

However, I made a big mistake. Instead of using the word "uma" which means "horse," I used the word "tsuma" which means "wife." When I said, "The cowboy rode into town on his wife and tied her up in front of the saloon," everyone began to giggle. I tried to continue the sermon, but several people were restraining their laughter, so I stopped the sermon and prayed. When I said, "Amen," they all roared with laughter.

When I thought about the fact that it took only one simple mistake to ruin my sermon, I became even more thankful that there are no mistakes in the Bible, for if there were even one mistake in the Bible, it would have an alarming effect on our faith.

Therefore, God gave us these words to strengthen our faith: "The words of the Lord are pure words." (Psalm 12:6) "Every word of God is pure." (Proverbs 30:5)

Missionaries who try to preach in Japanese may make many mistakes, but there are no mistakes in the Word they preach. The Bible is the perfect, inspired Word of God.

THE MIXED-UP MEMORY VERSE

The passage for my first sermon of the year was Second Corinthians 4:8-9. "We are troubled on every side, yet not distressed; we are perplexed, but not in despair; Persecuted, but not forsaken; cast down, but not destroyed."

I decided to make this passage the memory verse for this year and have everyone memorize it. I put the names of the members in a box, and every week after the service, I would pull out one name and have that member say the memory verse. Then we would all say it together.

One Sunday, one of the men did fine until he got to the middle of verse nine. Instead of saying, "Cast down, but not destroyed," he said, "Destroyed, but not cast down." Laughing, we all said, "That's wrong," and had him say it again.

Just as the passage says, there may be many times when the Christian is cast down, but he absolutely will not be destroyed. There are many Bible passages that teach this truth.

For example, in John 10:27-28 it is written, "My sheep hear my voice, and I know them, and they follow me: And I give unto them eternal life; and they shall never perish, neither shall any man pluck them out of my hand."

If verse nine were "destroyed, but not cast down," no Christian would laugh. However, over and over again in the Bible, the Lord promised, "They shall not be destroyed. They shall never perish." The life that God gives to us is just what the Bible says it is. It is eternal life.

THE MOST TERRIFYING WORD

This question was on a poll conducted in America: "To you, what is the most terrifying word?" Many people replied, "death" or "failure" or "debt." Interestingly, some people replied, "Marriage."

If you asked this question to students, they might reply "test." If you asked this question to a Japanese person, they would probably answer "earthquake" or "tsunami" or "typhoon." According to an ancient Japanese proverb, the four most terrifying things are earthquakes, lightning, fire and father.

According to the results of the poll, to many people, the most terrifying word is "cancer." Eighteen years ago, when the doctor said to me, "It is cancer," I was overwhelmed with fear.

Certainly, words like "death" or "earthquake" or "cancer" are terrifying, but in the Bible there are words much more terrifying than that. For example, in John 3:36 it is written, "He that believeth on the Son hath everlasting life: and he that believeth not the Son shall not see life; but the wrath of God abideth on him."

These words too are terrifying: "Whosoever was not found written in the book of life was cast into the lake of fire." (Revelation 20:15)

These words should have a profound effect on us. In Christians, they should produce a fervency to share the gospel with our family and friends. In people who have yet to believe in Christ, they should produce an intense desire to know how to be saved from the wrath of God and the lake of fire.

THE NAMES IN THE BASKET

Our memory verse for the Kokura church this year is Second Corinthians 4:8-9. I put the names of all the members on pieces of paper and put them in a basket. Every week we would draw one name out of the basket and that member would have to recite the verse.

One Sunday, I took all the names out of the basket and replaced them with names of Missionary Mike Winters on every paper. When his name was chosen, he was unable to recite the verse, so I chose another name out of the basket and that paper too had his name on it. He took the basket from me and saw that his name was on every paper. The members all roared with laughter.

I knew that Mike would try to get revenge sooner or later, so I checked the names in the basket every week. However, this past Sunday I forgot to check the names. When my name was chosen, I became suspicious. Sure enough, my name was written on every paper.

In Galatians 6:7 it is written, "Be not deceived; God is not mocked: for whatsoever a man soweth, that shall he also reap." I sowed seeds of mischief and reaped mischief.

Every day we sow seeds through our actions. Some people sow seeds of iniquity and wickedness. "They that plow iniquity, and sow wickedness, reap the same." (Job 4:8)

Of course, Christians should sow seeds of righteousness. "To him that soweth righteousness shall be a sure reward." (Proverbs 11:18) Will your harvest be a joyful harvest or a sorrowful harvest?

KEN BOARD

THE NEWSPAPER THAT
WOULD NOT GIVE UP

———— ⌐⌐ ————

The Ishinomaki Daily Newspaper began publication in 1913 and has printed the news for the people of Miyagi Prefecture for over 100 years. However, on March 11 of this year, this newspaper was placed in its most difficult circumstances. About 2:46 in the afternoon the building shook violently. The newspaper's computer was destroyed by the earthquake. The printing press was destroyed by the tidal wave that followed.

However, Mr. Takeuchi, the editor of the newspaper, and Mr. Omo, the publisher of the newspaper, did not give up. During the next three days, they continued their work in the cold building. There was no electricity, so with the aid of flashlights, they wrote the newspaper by hand. Usually, they distributed 14,000 copies of the newspaper daily. The day after the disaster, they delivered six hand-written copies of the paper to the community center and convenience store.

Their action caught the attention of the world. There were articles in the New York Times and Washington Post. Also, seven pages of the newspaper were exhibited at a museum in Washington. This newspaper that fulfilled its duty to inform everyone of the news in spite of the difficult situation is an example to all churches. In Mark 16:15 Christ commanded the church to go into all the world and preach the gospel to every creature. Even if "earthquakes" and "tidal waves" occur, let's continue to preach the gospel faithfully.

Mr. Takeuchi said, "What is important is not the size of the newspaper but the zeal of the newspaper." Let's put the word "church" in place of the word "newspaper" in this sentence. "It is not the size of the church that is important but the zeal of the church."

THE ONLY ONE LEFT STANDING

During December, I go to church every day about 4:30 and put out the stable scene – the stable (which is an inflatable balloon), Joseph, Mary, and baby Jesus in the manger. That day, the wind was extremely strong, so I checked on the stable set every thirty minutes.

A little after eight, I was working on a sermon when the doorbell ring. I opened the door and saw a mother holding a small child. She said, "It has fallen over." At first, I wasn't sure what she was talking about. When I realized she was talking about the stable set, I went to check on it. The stable had fallen over. Joseph had fallen over. Mary had fallen over. The only thing left standing was the baby Jesus doll in the manger.

As I stood there looking at that scene, I thought, "After all, when the storms of life attack us, the only one we can rely on is the Lord Jesus Christ." There are many righteous men like Joseph and many blessed women like Mary, but there is only one person who can save us from our sins. That one person is the one who was laid in that manger in Bethlehem – Jesus Christ. In Matthew 1:21 the Bible states that Jesus was born to "save his people from their sins."

Acts 4:12 declares that "neither is there salvation in any other: for there is none other name under heaven given among men, whereby we must be saved."

There never has been, neither will there ever be another person who can save us from our sins. "For there is one God, and one mediator between God and men, the man Christ Jesus; Who gave himself a ransom for all" (First Timothy 2:5-6)

THE POWER OF A KISS

According to the research of a doctor named Hajime Kimata, there is power in a kiss to decrease mental stress and suffering from allergies.

Couples who participated in his experiment kissed for thirty minutes while listening to soft music. The experiment showed that kissing lowered the level of the antibodies that caused allergic reactions. Dr Kimata's goal was to prove that our natural emotions have the power to decrease allergic reactions in people who are suffering from various allergies.

The Bible too exhorts kissing. There are four passages that command us to kiss one another in the letters that Paul wrote to churches. For example, in Romans 16:16 it is written, "Salute one another with an holy kiss." Peter included the same command in his first epistle. "Greet ye one another with a kiss of charity." (5:14) Until now, I have ignored this command, but beginning next Sunday, I intend to kiss each lady who comes to church. (Relax, ladies. It's just a joke.)

To the Christians of those days, kissing was a method of greeting. If Paul wrote a letter to present-day churches in Japan, he would probably write, "Greet one another with a holy bow." To the churches in America, he would write, "Greet one another with a holy handshake."

Of course, kissing is not merely a method of greeting. It is a method of expressing love to another person. What is important is not our method of greeting but showing love to one another, love based on God's holy love. "Love one another; as I have loved you, that ye also love one another." (John 13:34)

THE RING

When the earthquake happened on March 11, Mrs. Eriko Ohara put her two children, 5-year-old Ria and 2-year-old Rio, into the car and headed for a shelter. On the way she received a phone call from her husband, Yoshinari. "I am okay. The phone will go off shortly." There were many things that Eriko wanted to say to her husband, but she was unable to express her feelings. The phone cut off.

That phone call was their last conversation. Eriko was miraculously saved from the tidal wave, but her husband who was making deliveries did not make it. His body was found six days later. The next day Eriko went to the morgue. When she saw the body of her husband, she said with tears, "I love you."

Sometimes Eriko had criticized her husband. "I want you to give me a ring or something, but you are not the type of husband who gives presents to his wife." When she received the belongings of her husband from his company, she found a ring. On Valentine's Day she had given him some chocolate, so on the next Sunday, which was White Day, (a day when men give presents to the ladies who gave them chocolate on Valentine's Day), he intended to give her the ring. That ring was the symbol of his love to her.

Husbands, wives, what will you leave your wife or husband as a symbol of your love? Tomorrow you may not have the opportunity to tell them of your love, so tell them today through your words and your actions.

"Boast not thyself of tomorrow; for thou knowest not what a day may bring forth." (Proverbs 27:1)

THE RUPTURED POOL

Several people wanted to be baptized, so I searched for a pool we could use. One lady who comes to my English class said, "My husband will build you a pool." He built a pool exactly to the measurements that I requested, so I was extremely happy.

On Saturday night I went to church, filled the pool with water and returned home with great anticipation for the baptismal service on Sunday. On Sunday morning I went to church early to add some more water to the pool, but when I took the tarp off, my joy disappeared. The pool was empty. I had put too much water in the pool, so the water pressure had ruptured the pool in two places. We had to call off the baptismal service.

There are times when it seems like our heart is about to rupture because of the pressures of life. For example, our heart can be torn apart by financial problems or marriage difficulties or the loss of a job.

Paul and his co-laborers experienced this kind of pressure. In Second Corinthians 1:8 he wrote, "For we would not, brethren, have you ignorant of our trouble which came to us in Asia, that we were pressed out of measure, above strength, insomuch that we despaired even of life."

When we too are pressed to this extent, our heart may become empty like the church pool. In other words, there will be no joy or peace in our heart. When our heart is in this condition, let's remember the wonderful words in Isaiah 40:31. "They that wait upon the Lord shall renew their strength; they shall mount up with wings as eagles; they shall run, and not be weary; and they shall walk, and not faint."

THE SHOESHINE LADY

When you go to Tokyo, by all means, go to Shinbashi Station and have Mrs. Sachiko Nakamura shine your shoes. Mrs. Nakamura moved from Shizuoka to Tokyo sixty-six years ago. She soon married and had five children. She did various jobs to raise her children, but forty-five years ago, she began shining shoes near the train station in Shinbashi.

Because she wants to get the shoe polish into the tiny areas of the shoe, she puts the polish on her fingers and rubs it into the shoes. As a result, the fingerprint on the middle finger of her right hand has been worn away.

When asked the secret to working for as long as she had, she replied, "Good things won't happen every day at my job. But I guess the secret is to have faith that your hard work will pay off."

Christians who serve the Lord at church should pay heed to the words of Mrs. Nakamura. When we become tired and began to doubt if our service will have any effect at all, we should adopt her attitude. In other words, believing that there is benefit in continuing our service in the good times and in the bad times, let us be diligent in serving the Lord through our service at church.

Paul exhorted the same thing to the Christians in Corinth. "My beloved brethren, be ye stedfast, unmoveable, always abounding in the work of the Lord, forasmuch as ye know that your labour is not in vain in the Lord." (First Corinthians 15:58)

Also, he sent this exhortation to the believers in Galatia. "Let us not be weary in well doing: for in due season we shall reap, if we faint not." (Galatians 6:9)

THE SILENT MUSEUM

When I went to the town of Ueda in Nagano Prefecture, Pastor Ogawa of the Ueda Bible Baptist Church took me to an interesting museum called "The Silent Museum". This museum, which was opened during World War Two, is an art museum that displays paintings by artists who were killed during the war. Mr. Kuboshima, the owner of the museum, and a painter named Nomiyama went around the world collecting the paintings. Visitors to the museum observe the paintings that speak to them silently.

Christians are commanded to "go into all the world and preach the gospel to every creature." (Mark 16:15) Of course, the method of preaching is words.

However, there is one more method of spreading the gospel. It is a lifestyle in which the fruit of the Holy Spirit (love, joy, peace, longsuffering, gentleness, goodness, faith, meekness, and temperance) can be seen by others. (Galatians 5:22-23) Pastor Ogawa himself was led to Christ by the silent witness of a friend when he was a student at Kyushu University.

A winsome lifestyle that attracts the attention of people in our neighborhood and at our place of work can be a very effective method of evangelism. "Ye are the light of the world. A city that is set on an hill cannot be hid. Let your light so shine before men, that they may **see** your good works, and glorify your Father which is in heaven. (Matthew 5:14 and 16)

Let's preach the gospel with both our words and our good works.

THE SPIDER HOUSE

At one time, it had been a farmhouse. It was extremely old. The front entrance was a dirt floor and the walls were made of mud. Louise would clean the house, but if there were a strong wind, it looked like she had not cleaned for a month. However, it was near the church and had eight rooms, so our family of five happily moved into the house.

When we awoke the next morning, we found a huge spider in one of the glasses. When I say "huge," I mean really huge. That night we found another huge spider in the bathroom. We found out later that there were spiders living inside the walls. Every night huge spiders came out of the walls. Our children were afraid to go to the bathroom by themselves. I had to go first and check for spiders. I killed as many as I could, but after two years we gave up and moved to another house.

Just as my family and I lived in fear in a "Spider House," many people are living in a similar house of fear. In other words, their life is a life dominated by fear of somebody or something. Years ago, it was said that the four things Japanese fear the most are earthquakes, lightning, fires, and father. According to an Internet article, the things that modern-day Japanese fear the most are earthquakes, ghosts, fires, automobile accidents, lightning, and father.

If your heart is filled with fear, I urge you to move out of your "Spider House" and move into a house of faith in God.

If you do so, you too will be able to give the testimony that David gave in Psalm 27:1. "The Lord is my light and my salvation; whom shall I fear? the Lord is the strength of my life; of whom shall I be afraid?"

THE STORE CALLED "GOD"

Near my home there is a pet store named GOD. The first time I saw the store sign, I thought, "The owner of this store must have dyslexia. He meant to write DOG but wrote GOD."

One day I went to the store and asked, "Why did you name your pet store GOD?" The girl behind the counter replied, "Because the dog is God's favorite animal." I have heard the expression, "The dog is man's best friend," but I had never heard that the dog is God's favorite animal. There is no Bible verse that teaches that.

I found the names of over thirty animals in the King James Bible. These are the top ten animals mentioned the most: 1-Sheep (200 times); 2-Lambs (188); 3-Lions (176); 4-Cows (166); 5-Rams (165); 6-Horses (164); 7-Oxen (152); 8-Donkeys (150); 9-Goats (138); 10-Camels (62).

Dogs appear only forty-one times. But that's not all. Most of the time the Bible presents dogs as loathsome animals that we should avoid. In Philippians 3:2 we are warned to "beware of dogs" (the false teachers who preached "another gospel"). Also, in Second Peter 2:20-22 people who "have escaped the pollutions of the world through the knowledge of the Lord and Savior Jesus Christ" and then return to those pollutions are compared to a dog that returns to his own vomit.

Of course, dogs too are animals that were created by God, so God loves dogs too. However, He hates "dogs" who teach a way of salvation other than salvation by grace and faith. In Ephesians 2:8 the Bible makes it clear that we are saved "by grace through faith." Any person who teaches a gospel different from this is a "dog." Let's beware of them.

THE UNEXPECTED PRESENT

———— ❧ ————

For the past few weeks, I have had an upset stomach after I come home from church every Sunday. I thought the cause might be the soda bottle that I have been using for a water bottle for a long time, so I changed it to a new soda bottle.

When I told Brother and Sister Katoh about this, they said it would be better to use a thermos bottle, so when I went to the store on Monday, I intended to buy a thermos bottle, but I forgot.

That afternoon, something happened that surprised me. Every year there is a meeting for the elderly people in this area. I went last year, but I was unable to attend this year. After I returned from the grocery store, a lady from the neighborhood came to my house and said, "Mr. Board, since you were not able to come to the meeting for the elderly people, I brought you one of the presents that we gave to everyone." When I opened the present, I was surprised. It was a thermos bottle.

When I saw it, I remembered Matthew 6:31-32. "Therefore take no thought, saying, What shall we eat? or, What shall we drink? or, Wherewithal shall we be clothed? For your heavenly Father knoweth that ye have need of all these things." God supplied my need in an unexpected way.

The Bible teaches that God is concerned about even the small details of our life. According to Matthew 6:26-30, God feeds the birds of the air and clothes the lilies of the field. According to Luke 12:6, not one sparrow is forgotten before God. "Fear not therefore: ye are of more value than many sparrows." (Luke 12:7)

THE UPSIDE-DOWN GAUGE

I bought a new kerosene heater and brought it home and filled it with kerosene. When I checked the gauge the next day, I was somewhat surprised. The stove was almost empty. I brought the can of kerosene and began to put some into the stove. When I did, the kerosene spilled over on to the floor.

I looked at the gauge again. Although the gauge was all the way down to the bottom, the stove was full. Usually, as the stove uses up the kerosene, the gauge moves slowly toward the bottom. The gauge on the stove I bought was different. It was upside down. When the stove was full of kerosene, the gauge was at the bottom. As the stove used the kerosene, the gauge moved toward the top. When the stove was empty, the gauge was all the way up to the top. When the gauge was at the bottom, the stove was full.

That upside down gauge resembles our heart. When we become proud and lift ourselves up, our heart is empty of the grace of God. When we humble ourselves, our hearts will overflow with the grace of God. In James 4:6 it is written, "God resisteth the proud, but giveth grace unto the humble." In Luke 18:14 Christ said, "Every one that exalteth himself shall be abased; and he that humbleth himself shall be exalted."

Check the gauge of your heart. Is it at the top or the bottom? Is your heart a heart that is empty of the grace of God or a heart that is full of the grace of God? "Be clothed with humility: for God resisteth the proud, and giveth grace to the humble. Humble yourselves therefore under the mighty hand of God, that he may exalt you in due time." (First Peter 5:5-6)

THE WELL

Before construction begins on a new building in Japan, a Shinto priest comes and performs a ceremony to purify the ground. When Christians construct a church, they do not conduct this ceremony, but for the concern of the workers who are usually all non-Christian, we perform a ceremony to pray for the safety of the workers who will build the building.

A well on the Kokura church property was a concern for the workers because they believe that the god of water lives in wells. Of course, Christians believe that there is only one true God, but for the peace of mind for the carpenters and other workers, I stood on the covering of the well and prayed a prayer asking God to drive away all spirits in the well and on the property.

Different from the wells in Japanese superstitions, wells that appear in the Bible are not fearsome things but joyful things. One day, Christ became weary during a journey and sat on the side of a well. A woman came to the well to draw water. Christ said to her, "Whosoever drinketh of this water shall thirst again: But whosoever drinketh of the water that I shall give him shall never thirst; but the water that I shall give him shall be in him a well of water springing up into everlasting life." (John 4:13-14) When a person believes in Christ, He puts a well of living water in his heart.

This is the chorus of one of my favorite hymns, "Springs of Living Water." "Drinking at the springs of living water, Happy now am I, my soul they satisfy; Drinking at the springs of living water, O wonderful and bountiful supply."

THE WISE DOG

One of the ladies of the church is raising a dog named Samuel. Until recently, whenever she went upstairs in her home, Samuel went with her. However, one day he went up the stairs just a little way, stopped, and then quickly returned to the bottom of the stairs. Even if she called, "Samuel, come here," he would go just a little way up the stairs, stop, and then go back to the bottom of the stairs.

She wondered why Samuel had stopped going upstairs. She checked his claws and discovered that they had gotten longer, so when he tried to climb the stairs, he sensed he was in danger of slipping. That is why he would not climb the stairs anymore.

I wonder if we have as much wisdom as Samuel. In other words, when we realize we are walking on a dangerous road, do we have enough wisdom to stop and return to a safe place? In Psalm 73:2 Asaph expressed this dangerous condition in these words: "But as for me, my feet were almost gone; my steps had well nigh slipped."

When we realize that we have departed from the way of the Lord and are walking on a slippery road, what should we do? Like Samuel, let us return to a safe place, the place where we departed from the way of the Lord and once more walk in the way that the Lord leads us. Let us follow the example of David. "I have refrained my feet from every evil way, that I might keep thy word." Psalm 119:101)

In Proverbs 14:12 it is written, "There is a way which seemeth right unto a man, but the end thereof are the ways of death." Are you certain that the road on which you are walking is a safe road?

THE WORD I HATE

Recently once again I had to say the word that I hate. It was when I took my friend's family who are going to America to the airport. When she returns to Japan, she probably will not come back to Kyushu, so I may never meet her on this earth again. I was sad as I watched them walk away.

The word that I hate is "Goodbye." Every time I return to America and have to say "sayonara" to my family and friends in Japan, my heart is filled with sadness. And then, every time I return to Japan and have to say "Goodbye" to my family and friends in America, I am crying when I board the airplane.

However, according to the Bible, some day we will go to a land where no one will say "Goodbye." This is the chorus of a song entitled "The Land of No Goodbyes."

[Goodbyes won't be spoken, no hearts will be broken
Not a tear to dim our eyes over loved ones who have died
We'll be together with family and friends
We'll never have to part again
When we reach that land of no goodbyes]

Hallelujah! The time is coming when we will not have to say "Goodbye" any more. "For the Lord Himself will descend from heaven with a shout, with the voice of an archangel, and with the trumpet of God. And the dead in Christ will rise first. Then we who are alive and remain shall be caught up together with them in the clouds to meet the Lord in the air. And thus we shall always be with the Lord. Therefore comfort one another with these words." (First Thessalonians 4:16-18)

KEN BOARD

THE $100 SPIDER

The instant I stepped into the shower room, I noticed two things. First, the window was open about two inches. Second, there was a huge spider on the wall. I splashed some water on the spider, so it escaped through the open window. I relaxed and took my shower.

As I turned to leave the room, I noticed another huge spider on the floor between me and the door. I splashed water on the spider, but he did not move. I picked up the small stool that everyone sits on to wash off before they get into the bathtub and threw it at the spider. The stool hit the spider, but then it bounced off the floor and hit the glass door. The spider was dead, but it cost me $100 to repair the door.

Because I left the window open just a little, I ended up having to pay $100. In the same way, the Christian who leaves the door of his heart open when he leaves the house may end up suffering loss. The heart of the Christian who does not read the Bible daily is an open heart through which temptations can enter. To make certain we do not yield to those temptations, we can follow the example of David. "Thy word have I hid in mine heart, that I might not sin against thee." (Psalm 119:11)

Also, the heart of the Christian who does not pray daily is an open heart through which anxiety and discontent can enter. To prevent this, let us remember the exhortation in Philippians 4:6-7. "In every thing by prayer and supplication with thanksgiving let your requests be made known unto God. And the peace of God, which passeth all understanding, shall keep your hearts and minds through Christ Jesus."

Beware of the "spiders" who are searching for a way to enter our heart.

THEIR LAST WORDS

"A 30-foot tidal wave is coming! Evacuate to a high place!" With these words 52-year-old Takeshi Miura and 24-year-old Miki Endo, who were working in the ward office at South Sanrikucho, warned the people of the town. From the time the earthquake took place until the tidal wave came, the two of them continued to repeat the warning over the ward office loudspeaker.

When the tidal wave came, Miss Endo said to her co-worker, "Takeshi, that's enough. Let go up to the roof." He replied, "Let's announce it just one more time." At that time, they were on the second floor of the ward office. Both of them are still missing.

Many people were saved through the last words of Mr. Miura and Miss Endo. Among those who were saved were Mr. Miura's wife, Hiromi, and Miss Endo's mother, Mieko. Hiromi said to her dead husband, "Your voice saved the lives of many people." Many people of the town thanked Mieko. "Your daughter's warning saved us."

The last words of Christ saved many people too. He said to His disciples, "Go ye into all the world, and preach the gospel to every creature." (Mark 16:15) Those who were saved through the evangelism of the disciples went from town to town and country to country and preached the gospel. The evangelism that began with the last words of Christ brought salvation to many people. The last words of Christ are words that were also spoken to us who are living today. Like Mr. Miura and Miss Endo, let's remain at our post and preach the gospel faithfully until the very end. "Preach the word; be instant in season, out of season." (Second Timothy 4:2)

THEY THOUGHT I WAS COLONEL SANDERS

Has anyone ever told you, "You look like So-and-So?" Since I came to Japan, many times I have been told that I look like Colonel Sanders of Kentucky Fried Chicken.

Until recently I did not think that I resembled him; however, the other day when I went to KFC, something quite interesting happened. While I was waiting for my order, I was standing by the statue of Colonel Sanders. Two young men walked toward me. When they saw me and the statue of Colonel Sanders, they were so amazed that they just stared at me. I asked, "Do I look like him?" They replied, "You look exactly like him," and then they asked, "May we take your picture?" I laughed while they took a picture of me and Colonel Sanders.

When I am told that I resemble Colonel Sanders, I do not know whether or not to take it as a compliment. After all, the statue is the statue of an old, fat man.

I am a Christian who is trying to follow the footprints of Christ, so what I would really like to be told is, "You resemble Christ." According to the Bible, this is something that God desires of all Christians. "For whom he did foreknow, he also did predestinate to be conformed to the image of his Son, that he might be the firstborn among many brethren." (Romans 8:29)

The purpose of everything that happens in our life is the work of the Lord to conform us to the image of Christ. You may not be pleased if someone says, "You look like Colonel Sanders,' but if anyone ever tells you, "You- look like Jesus," consider it the highest compliment for a Christian.

THINGS THAT DO NOT
GO TOGETHER

———— ❧ ————

I got into the car, put my ETC card into the ETC device and turned on the engine. There was a strange, ear-piercing sound. Missionary Mike Wyatt and I were both startled. I tried turning off the engine and turning it on again. We heard the same ear-piercing sound. Mike and I checked all the gauges. They were normal.

I took out the ETC card and the noise stopped. When I looked at the card, I discovered the cause of the sound. The card that I inserted into the ETC device was not the ETC card. It was my credit card. Please remember this: ETC devices and credit cards do not go together.

According to the Bible, there are actions that resemble putting a credit card into an ETC device. First, blessing God with our mouth and using the same mouth to speak evil of others are two actions that do not go together. "Therewith bless we God, even the Father; and therewith curse we men, which are made after the similitude of God. Out of the same mouth proceedeth blessing and cursing. My brethren, these things ought not so to be." (James 3:9-10)

Also, trying to serve God and something else at the same time are two actions that do not go together. "No man can serve two masters: for either he will hate the one, and love the other; or else he will hold to the one, and despise the other. Ye cannot serve God and mammon." (Matthew 6:24)

One more: Christians and non-Christians do not go together in marriage. "Be ye not unequally yoked together with unbelievers: for what fellowship hath righteousness with unrighteousness?" (Second Corinthians 6:14)

THIRTY-SIX DAYS OF MEALS

I do not know how to cook, so when my wife went home to be with the Lord, daily meals were a big problem. Thankfully, supermarkets and convenience stores sell delicious meals that can be cooked in a microwave oven, so I have managed to get by with those for the past seven years.

There are days, however, when I want to eat some of the "home cooking" that my wife used to make. Happily, right now my freezer and refrigerator are filled with "home cooking." The other day, when missionary Mike Winters and I were distributing flyers, his wife, Cristy, prepared enough meals for me for thirty-six days! She prepared six spaghetti meals, ten chicken enchilada meals, six grilled chicken meals and fourteen hamburger meals. While they are on furlough, I will still be able to enjoy Cristy's delicious meals.

Each day, when I open the freezer and see the meals Cristy prepared for me, I am reminded of the things God has prepared for people who believe in Christ. For example, He has prepared a home for us. In John 14:2 Jesus said, "In my Father's house are many mansions: if it were not so, I would have told you. I go to prepare a place for you."

Also, according to Hebrews 11:16 and Revelation 21:2, He has prepared a beautiful city for us.

I would like to tell you more about the things God has prepared for us, but I can't, for in First Corinthians 2:9 it is written, "Eye hath not seen, nor ear heard, neither have entered into the heart of man, the things which God hath prepared for them that love him."

THREE HOURS AT THE WARD OFFICE

————— ❧ —————

On Monday of last week, missionary Mike Wyatt and I went to the South Kokura Ward Office to register his family for the Japan health insurance system. First, we went to the health insurance window and received a number. There were many people at the Ward Office that day, so we waited a long time. Finally, our number was called; however, we were told that first we had to go to a different window and register.

We went to that window, took a number and waited a long time. When our number was finally called, the Ward Office official told us that the registration process would take a long time. We waited at that window for one hour and twenty-five minutes.

Then we returned to the health insurance window and waited a long time. We arrived at the Ward Office at one o'clock and left there at four o'clock. It was a long, long three hours. As we were leaving the Ward Office, I said to Mike, "It is easier to get into heaven than it is to get into the Japan health system."

I was joking, but it really is true. There are three things a person has to do to get into heaven. First, admit your sins to God and repent. Second, believe that Jesus Christ died on the cross for your sins. Third, pray to God and ask Him to forgive your sins.

In Luke 18:13 there is the story of a sinful man who prayed this simple prayer. "God, be merciful to me a sinner." What happened when he prayed that simple prayer? In verse 14 it is written, "This man went down to his house justified." It is simple. Go ahead. Give it a try. It is a lot easier than registering for the Japan health system.

THREE PILLARS FOR LIVING POWER

In the February 15th edition of the Asahi Newspaper there was an article entitled "Three Pillars for Living Power." (This is a summary of that article.) Because schools want to foster the power to live in students, the purpose of education will continue to be three things: 1-Knowledge and skill; 2-Intellectual power and the power of judgment and expression; 3-The power to learn.

These three pillars that give students the power to live are also necessary for Christians who want to grow spiritually.

1-Knowledge. In Philippians 1:9 Paul wrote, "This I pray, that your love may abound yet more and more <u>in knowledge</u> and in all judgment."

2-Thought. "Whatsoever things are true, whatsoever things are honest, whatsoever things are just, whatsoever things are pure, whatsoever things are lovely, whatsoever things are of good report; if there be any virtue, and if there be any praise, think on these things." (Philippians 4:8)

3-Learning. In Matthew 11:28-29 Christ said, "Come unto me, all ye that labour and are heavy laden, and I will give you rest. Take my yoke upon you, and <u>learn of me</u>; for I am meek and lowly in heart: and ye shall find rest unto your souls."

The three pillars of the Christian who desires to live a powerful life for God are obtaining true knowledge through reading the Word of God daily, thinking rightly through the assistance of the Holy Spirit, and learning from Christ Himself through intimate fellowship with Him in our daily life.

THREE SECONDS

Lately there have been two incidents that taught me the importance of three seconds. First, I had lunch at a soba shop near the church. The cook told me that as soon as he puts the soba noodles into the water, he sets a timer for exactly 13 seconds. 10 seconds is too short, and 16 seconds is too long. In order to serve his customers the most delicious soba, he has to take the noodles out of the water after exactly 13 seconds.

When he serves the soba to the customer, he wants the customer to begin eating immediately. Before I began eating, I prayed and thanked the Lord for my meal. I could tell he was disappointed. I promised him, "Next time I will pray before I come."

The other incident took place when I was on my way home from shopping. As I neared the intersection, a car driven by a young lady came through the intersection at a high speed. Not only did she ignore the stop sign, she went through the intersection at a very dangerous speed. If I had been three seconds earlier, I would have been involved in a terrible car accident and maybe even killed.

When I realized how close to death I had come, I remembered the words of David in First Samuel 20:3. "There is but a step between me and death." In my case, it was not one step but three seconds. There were only three seconds between me and death.

My experience reminded me of the uncertainty of life. When I go through the next intersection, when I go around the next curve, I do not know what will happen in the next three seconds. Therefore, in Amos 4:12 the Bible urges us to prepare to meet the Lord.

KEN BOARD

TOMATO RAMEN

I had a phone call from my son. "Dad, I found a new restaurant. It's very delicious." "Oh, what's the name of the restaurant?" "It's Tomato Ramen." "What? Tomato Ramen ?" "Yes, the flavor of the ramen soup is tomato. It's very delicious."

To be honest, when I heard that the flavor of the soup was tomato, one word came to my mind. "Yuck!" I did not want to eat tomato ramen. When I went to Kagoshima, my son took me to "Tomato Ramen." I really was not looking forward to it. However, when I ate tomato ramen, I was surprised. It was delicious. It was the best ramen I have ever eaten. The soup was so delicious that I lifted the bowl to my mouth and drank every drop of it.

When I first heard "Tomato Ramen," I thought, "Tomato Ramen? It's not delicious. I don't want to eat it." However, when I tasted it, I discovered that it was quite delicious. In the same way, when some people hear the words "God" or "Bible", their reaction is, "God? I don't want Him. Bible? It's not interesting." However, when we taste God and the Bible which is the Word of God, we find that they are very delicious. In Psalm 34:8 it is written, "O taste and see that the LORD is good: blessed is the man that trusteth in him."

The life of the person who lives each day in fellowship with the living God is a delightful life. The Word of God is delicious too. "How sweet are thy words unto my taste! yea, sweeter than honey to my mouth!" (Psalm 119:103) Please taste the wonderfulness of God and the delicious words of the Bible. If you will do so, you will exclaim as I did when I ate tomato ramen for the first time. "It's delicious!"

TOO OLD?

❧

Momofuku Ando invented Ramen Noodles when he was sixty-one years old. Tamae Watanabe climbed Mount Everest at the age of seventy-three. Minoru Saito sailed around the world at the age of seventy-seven. Yuuichiro Mimura climbed Mount Everest at the age of eighty. Seiichi Igarashi climbed Mount Fuji at the age of one hundred!

These people did not consider themselves too old to accomplish these feats. They lived lives that were not restricted by their ages.

Last month, when I preached at the graduation service of Japan Baptist Bible College, these people came to my mind. Many people think that Bible College is a place where young people go to receive training to become pastors or missionaries. However, two of the students who graduated last month were fifty years old and forty years old.

The Bible relates the stories of several elderly people who were used greatly by the Lord. For example, Moses was eighty years old when he was chosen by God to lead the people of Israel out of Egypt (Exodus 3). Abraham was seventy-five years old when God commanded him to leave his home and go to the land which God would show to him (Genesis 12). Caleb was eighty-five years old when he conquered the land that God had given him in the Promised Land (Joshua 14). It is thought that John was about ninety years old when he wrote the book of Revelation.

We never get TOO OLD to serve the Lord. No matter how old we become, let us pray the prayer in Psalm 71:18. "Now also when I am old and greyheaded, O God, forsake me not; until I have shewed thy strength unto this generation, and thy power to every one that is to come."

KEN BOARD

"TRY IT. YOU'LL LIKE IT!"

When I had dinner at the house of a friend, he urged me to try a hot sauce. "This sauce is delicious. Try it." I like spicy food, but I do not care for spicy sauces like Tabasco. The sauce he urged me to try was the same color as Tabasco and it had "SOS' written on the bottle, so I decided that sauce was too spicy for me and declined.

Later his wife urged me to try it. "It is not that spicy. Try just a little." I put some of it on my food and tasted it. It was delicious! After that, I put it on everything I ate.

Often people judge food with their eyes and refuse to eat it. I often did that when I first went to Japan. Later, when I tried those foods, I discovered that they were quite delicious (most of them).

Regretfully, just as some people refuse to try some foods, some people reject God without even getting to know Him. Likewise, some people decide that the Bible is not interesting without even trying to read it. Although they have never been to church, they judge church to be boring.

Sometimes when people refuse to eat a certain food without even trying it, we say, "Try it. You'll like it!" To the person who rejects God without even knowing what kind of God He is, I say, "Try Him. You'll like Him!"

In Psalm 34:8 it is written, "O taste and see that the LORD is good: blessed is the man that trusteth in him." Those who have already "tasted" the Lord had found that He is a gracious God. (First Peter 2:3) Try it. Draw near to God. Read the Bible. Go to church. If you will do so, you will rejoice as I did when I finally tried the spicy-looking sauce.

TWO HELLS

───────── ❧ ─────────

Last Monday, a friend and I went to a place called Hell in Beppu. The Hell in Beppu definitely resembles the Hell described in the Bible. The temperature in the pond is 100 degrees. It is a literal lake of fire. Also, the smell of brimstone (sulfur) was strong. (Revelation 20:12-15)

However, there are two big differences in the Hell of the Bible and the Hell in Beppu. First of all, there are exits in the Hell in Beppu. There are entrances and exits in all seven of the Hells in Beppu. Before we went to Beppu, my friend asked jokingly, "Will we be able to come back?" Yes, you can enter and leave the Hell in Beppu. However, there is no exit in the Hell of the Bible. There is only an entrance.

In Luke 16:26 Christ spoke these words to a man who went to Hell. "Between us and you there is a great gulf fixed: so that they which would pass from hence to you cannot; neither can they pass to us, that would come from thence." According to Revelation 14:11, the torment of the people who go to Hell is an everlasting torment.

There is another big difference. My friend and I visited all seven of the Hells in Beppu, and wherever we went, people were having a good time. They were taking pictures, eating, drinking and laughing. However, the people who go to the Hell described in the Bible will do none of those things. They will weep and gnash their teeth. (Matthew 25:30)

If you ever have the chance to go to the Hell in Beppu, please go. It is an interesting place. However, I plead with you with all of my heart. Please do not go to the Bible Hell. Believe in Jesus who died on the cross to save you from that awful place,

TWO LEFT SHOES

I bought two pairs of new shoes while I was in America. I sent one pair of shoes to Japan and kept one pair with me to wear when I went to church. On Sunday morning I opened the box of shoes and noticed something that upset me terribly. The two shoes that I had sent to Japan were both shoes for the right foot. The two shoes that I had kept in America were both shoes for the left foot. There was nothing to do but to wear my old shoes to church.

Two shoes for the left foot are not any help at all. According to the Bible, there are two actions that resemble trying to wear two left shoes. First of all, the action of trying to become righteous before God by your own good works is similar to trying to wear two left shoes. In Romans 3:20 it is written, "By the deeds of the law there shall be no flesh be justified in his sight." Also, according to Ephesians 2:8-9, we are saved by God's grace through faith in Christ, not by works.

After a person becomes a Christian, trying to depend on your own strength to live a Christian life is similar to trying to wear two left shoes. In John 15:5 Christ said, "I am the vine, ye are the branches: He that abideth in me, and I in him, the same bringeth forth much fruit: for without me ye can do nothing."

The person who can live a faithful Christian life is the person who has daily fellowship with Christ through the Bible and prayer. In Philippians 4:13 it is written, "I can do all things through Christ which strengtheneth me." The person who is trying to go to heaven by his own good works and the Christian who is trying by his own power to live a life that is pleasing to the Lord are both trying to wear two left shoes.

TWO PIECES OF PAPER

———— ❧ ————

In my wallet there is some money and two pieces of paper. I carry one piece of those papers to protect me from the police.

When I went to the immigration office to renew my visa, the official said, "Your visa expired three months ago. You are living in Japan illegally right now. The police may come to arrest you." He handed me a document and said, "If the police come, show them this document." I put that document in my wallet. Now, whenever I leave the house, I make sure I have my wallet with me.

The purpose of one of the papers in my wallet is to protect me from the police. The purpose of the other piece of paper is to protect me from the attacks of the devil. On August 3, 1955 I received Jesus Christ as my personal Savior. According to many passages in the Bible, when I did that, I received eternal life. In Romans 6:23 it is written, "For the wages of sin is death; but the gift of God is eternal life through Jesus Christ our Lord."

Since that day in 1955, many times the devil has tried to make me doubt my salvation. When I stumble and do something that is not pleasing to the Lord, immediately he will come and whisper, "You say you are a Christian, but a true Christian would not do what you just did."

When that happens, I take out the other piece of paper in my wallet and read it. This is what is written on that piece of paper. "Verily, verily, I say unto you, He that heareth my word, and believeth on him that sent me, hath everlasting life, and shall not come into condemnation; but is passed from death unto life." (John 5:24)

TWO TOY CARS

If you came to my home, you might notice something strange. There are two toy cars on my desk. One is a white 8-passenger van. The other one is a yellow monster truck. When I went to America last year, I received the yellow monster truck from my grandson, Josiah. It was one of his favorite toy cars, but he gave it to me. Now, whenever I look at that toy car, I remember Josiah.

My grandson, Noah, who lives in Kagoshima, gave the white van to me. That toy car looked just like my car, so Noah said, "Grandpa, this toy car looks like your car, so I will give it to you." Now, whenever I look at that toy car, I remember Noah.

Today is the day that Christians celebrate the resurrection of Christ. Just as Josiah and Noah gave me their toy trucks to remember them, Christ left us three things for us to remember Him. First, He left us an empty tomb. "The angel answered and said unto the women, Fear not ye: for I know that ye seek Jesus, which was crucified. He is not here: for he is risen." (Matthew 28:5-6)

Second, in John 11:25-26 Christ left us a wonderful promise. "I am the resurrection, and the life: he that believeth in me, though he were dead, yet shall he live. And whosoever liveth and believeth in me shall never die."

Third, Christ left us a living hope. "Blessed be the God and Father of our Lord Jesus Christ, which according to his abundant mercy hath begotten us again unto a lively hope by the resurrection of Jesus Christ from the dead." (First Peter 1:3)

UNDEFEATED!

———— ❧ ————

Did you hear about the perfect record? No, not the perfect record of sumo grand champion Harumafuji. MY perfect record.

Since 2003, I have participated in SUMO GAME, an online game for fans of sumo. Just like real sumo wrestlers, we all have a professional wrestling name. My name is KIBOOYAMA which means "mountain of hope." Each day during the 15 days of the sumo tournament, my opponent and I choose ten wrestlers that we think will win that day. Whoever chooses the most winners wins the match.

I have been playing this game for 10 years, but I am still in the lower division. However, this tournament I have not lost once during the first 14 days. On the 15th day, the first two wrestlers that I had chosen both lost, so I was discouraged. It did not look like I would have a perfect record. In order for me to win, both of my opponent's final two wrestlers would have to lose. Both of them lost, so I won the championship with a perfect 15-0 record. In the history of the Sumo Game, I am only the second person to finish undefeated.

The Christian life is not a game, but like sumo, it is a life of victory and defeat. There are times when we win and there are times when we lose. When we give in to temptation and sin, we are discouraged. We think that it is impossible to live a life of victory, but we must not quit. According to Romans 8:37, we can become "more than conquerors" through faith in Christ. If we trust not in our own power but in the power of the Lord, we can live a victorious life. "For whatsoever is born of God overcometh the world: and this is the victory that overcometh the world, even our faith." (First John 5:4)

WATCH OUT!

———— ❧ ————

Pastor Sakai and I are fans of the Softbank Hawks. When he returned to Kyushu last week, I learned that, although he has been rooting for the Hawks for many years, he had never been to one of their games, so I took him to a game at Yahoo Dome. (The Hawks won 5-0.)

Whenever a foul ball went into the stands, there would be this announcement in Japanese: "Watch out for foul balls." Then, about five seconds later, there would be the announcement, "Watch out!" in English. I found this quite interesting because the English announcement usually came after the ball had already entered the stands, so between the Japanese announcement and the English announcement, I would yell out, "Watch out!" Pastor Sakai was laughing at me the entire game.

Christians who are trying to walk the right path do not have to worry about foul balls, but in the Bible we can find several passages warning us to watch out. For example, because we do not know when the second coming of Christ will take place, we are warned to constantly live a life that is pleasing to the Lord. "Take ye heed, watch and pray: for ye know not when the time is." (Mark 13:33)

Also, we are urged to watch out in order to stand against the many wiles of the devil. "Praying always with all prayer and supplication in the Spirit, and watching thereunto with all perseverance and supplication for all saints." (Ephesians 6:18)

Finally, in one of His greatest statements concerning human weakness, Jesus said, "Watch and pray, that ye enter not into temptation: the spirit indeed is willing, but the flesh is weak." (Matthew 26:41)

WHAT DO I DO WITH THE CAKE?

─────────── ❧ ───────────

Lately everyone at church has been greeting one another with these words: "It's cold!" It definitely is cold, especially when the wind is blowing. I do not have a heater in my bedroom, but there is one in the living room, so I have been sleeping there on a futon lately.

On Thursday I bought a large cake for our Christmas party. I intended to keep it in the refrigerator until Sunday, but it was too big for my refrigerator. I wondered, "What can I do with the cake until Sunday?" The solution to this problem was simple. I put the cake in my bedroom, for it is as cold in there as it is in the refrigerator.

As I considered the cold weather, it seemed to manifest the spiritual condition of Japan. Even if the church distributes thousands of flyers, no new people will come. Even if we plan a fun-filled program for children, not many children will come.

As we try to spread the gospel in this spiritual coldness, we must be aware of three dangers. First, we must not become lazy. "The sluggard will not plow by reason of the cold; therefore shall he beg in harvest, and have nothing." (Proverbs 20:4)

Second, we must not let the results of our evangelism discourage us. In spite of the cold hearts of so many people, may our feet be not cold feet but feet that "preach the gospel of peace, and bring glad tidings of good things!" (Romans 10:15)

Third, even though our bodies are cold, we must not let our hearts become cold and lose our passion for evangelism.

KEN BOARD

WHAT! RED IS "ON" AND GREEN IS "OFF"!

———— ❧ ————

When I attended the BBF Global Meeting held in Korea, one night I was asked to serve as an interpreter. When I sat in front of the microphone, I noticed a red button and a green button, so I assumed the red button was the OFF button and the green button was the ON button. When it was time for me to interpret, I turned on the green button. When I was not interpreting, I turned on the red button and talked to the person sitting next to me.

However, as I was to find out later, the red button was the ON button and the green button was the OFF button. Instead of listening to my interpretation of what was being said on the platform, nearly fifty Japanese heard my conversation with the person sitting next to me! Later, when they were laughing at me, I replied, "Anyone would think that the red button was the OFF button and the green button was the ON button."

Sometimes, when we read the Bible, our feeling is the same feeling as mine when I found out that the red button was the ON button and the green button was the OFF button. For example, we read Matthew 16:25 and we think, "What! That can't be right." Jesus said, "For whosoever will save his life shall lose it: and whosoever will lose his life for my sake shall find it." Usually, we struggle with all our might to save our life, but according to Christ, we save our life when we lose it for the Lord's sake.

There is another example in Second Corinthians 12:10. "When I am weak, then am I strong." What! I am strong when I am weak? Yes, when we realize our weakness and trust in the power of the Lord, it is then that we become strong.

WHAT IS YOUR MOUNT FUJI?

— ❧ —

I will remember April 6, 1968 until the day the Lord calls me home. Having just arrived in Japan for the first time three days earlier, my family and I boarded a flight for Fukuoka. On the way, the pilot made an announcement that excited everyone. "You can see Mount Fuji on the left side of the plane." Covered in snow, Mount Fuji was shining. Until this day, the most beautiful natural sight that I have ever seen is the scene of Mount Fuji that day.

There is a 69-year-old man in Shizuoka Prefecture who has climbed Mount Fuji 1450 times! The record is 1672 times, so to break that record, he climbs Mount Fuji 200 times each year. Sometimes he climbs it twice in one day! Although almost all Japanese would like to climb Mount Fuji at least once, many of them will never be able to make that dream come true. I climbed part way up the mountain once, but I have never climbed all the way to the top.

Even though I am not able to climb Mount Fuji, I can climb the "Mount Fuji" of my life. The "Mount Fuji" of my life is the goal for which I aiming. Of course, the Mount Fuji of each person will be different. That which each person wants to accomplish in his life is the Mount Fuji of that person.

I urge each Christian to decide on your Mount Fuji and pursue it diligently like the apostle Paul did. "This one thing I do, forgetting those things which are behind, and reaching forth unto those things which are before, I press toward the mark for the prize of the high calling of God in Christ Jesus." (Philippians 3:13-14) Once we decide the "Mount Fuji" of our life, let us climb that mountain diligently.

WHAT IS YOUR NAME?

My name is BOARD. There are not many people named Board in the United States. According to the census in the year 2000, the five most popular names in the United States are Smith, Johnson, Williams, Brown and Jones. There are over 2,300,000 Americans named Smith, but only 3,856 people named Board. Board ranked number 7959 on the list. Actually, there are more people named Nakamura than people named Board in the United States,

Here are the most popular Japanese names in order of rank: 1-Satoh 2-Suzuki 3-Takahashi 4-Tanaka 5-Watanabe 6-Itoh 7-Yamamoto 8-Nakamura 9-Kobayashi 10-Saitoh.

Is you name on this list? A more important question is, "Is your name written in the Book of Life" "I saw the dead, small and great, stand before God; and the books were opened: and another book was opened, which is the book of life: and the dead were judged out of those things which were written in the books, according to their works." (Revelation 29:12)

The Book of Life is a list of all the names of people who believed in the Savior Jesus Christ.

What will happen to people whose names are not written in the Book of Life? There terrible words in Revelation 20:15 answer that question: "Whosoever was not found written in the book of life was cast into the lake of fire."

If you have already believed in Christ, rejoice. "In this rejoice not, that the spirits are subject unto you; but rather rejoice, because your names are written in heaven." (Luke 10:20)

WHAT WAS THE DIFFERENCE?

Last year, when I went to Nagashima, Pastor Kishimoto's granddaughter, Ai, let me hold her. (Ai means "love" in Japanese.) However, this year, no matter how many times I held out my arms to her, she would not come to me.

However, I did not give up. I thought if I could make her laugh, she would lose her fear and come to me. I made all kinds of funny faces and made funny sounds with my mouth, but she would not come to me

After the evening service, I tried again. I made funny faces and funny sounds again and tried to get her to talk to me. This time she laughed and talked with me. What was the difference between Ai in the afternoon and Ai in the evening? In the afternoon, her mother was holding her. In the evening, her father was holding her. When her father was holding her, she was no longer afraid of me.

It is the same with Christians. When we are conscious of the fact that our heavenly Father is with us, we become courageous Christians. In Deuteronomy 31:6 it is written, "Be strong and of a good courage, fear not, nor be afraid of them: for the Lord thy God, he it is that doth go with thee; he will not fail thee, nor forsake thee." When we are conscious of this truth, the truth that our heavenly Father is always with us, we have the courage to live a lifestyle that is different from the lifestyle of this world.

When Jesus said, "Go ye therefore, and teach all nations," immediately He added these words, "I am with you always." The Christian who believes this is able to share the gospel with others without fear.

WHEN IT RAINS, IT POURS

There is a Japanese proverb – *fureba doshaburi da* – which means, "When it rains, it pours." There is a similar expression in English – "Bad luck always comes in threes." On Friday of last week. I learned that this proverb is true.

First, my toilet broke. When I flushed it, the water would not stop running. I had to cut off the water until I could have the toilet repaired.

Next, I had planned to go shopping, but the car would not move. The battery was dead, so I had to have it recharged.

Then, about three o'clock in the afternoon, my air conditioner stopped cooling. The temperature was about ninety-five that day, so I had to get by with just a fan until the air conditioner started cooling again.

When the bad things started piling up, I began to feel a little bit like Job; however, his experience was much worse.

First, all his oxen and asses were taken by his enemies. Next, fire fell from heaven and burned up all his sheep. Then, a great wind collapsed the house where his ten children were gathered and they all died.

When I had my bad day, I felt like complaining, but Job did not complain. Instead, he said, "Naked came I out of my mother's womb, and naked shall I return thither: the LORD gave, and the LORD hath taken away; blessed be the name of the LORD." (Job 1:21) Pray that we too will become Christians who can say the same thing when misfortunes begin to pile up.

WHEN VICTORY BECAME A DEFEAT

───────── ❧ ─────────

Last month, the super flyweight boxing championship was held in Osaka. The champion, Kameda Daiki, faced Liborio Solis from Venezuela. Solis won by a 2-1 decision, but he did not become champion. At the weigh-in the previous day, his weight was over the super flyweight limit, so although he defeated Kameda, because he broke the rules, he did not become champion.

When I read this article in the newspaper, two Bible passages came to my mind. First, Second Timothy 2:5. "If a man also strive for masteries, yet is he not crowned, except he strive lawfully."

The other passage is a parable of Jesus. "And he spake a parable unto them, saying, The ground of a certain rich man brought forth plentifully: And he thought within himself, saying, What shall I do, because I have no room where to bestow my fruits? And he said, This will I do: I will pull down my barns, and build greater; and there will I bestow all my fruits and my goods. And I will say to my soul, Soul, thou hast much goods laid up for many years; take thine ease, eat, drink, and be merry. But God said unto him, Thou fool, this night thy soul shall be required of thee: then whose shall those things be, which thou hast provided? So is he that layeth up treasure for himself, and is not rich toward God."

The rich man appeared to be successful, but the Lord said he was a failure. He made provision for his flesh but made no provision for his soul. In Mark 8:36 Jesus said, "For what shall it profit a man, if he shall gain the whole world, and lose his own soul?"

The person who satisfies the needs of his body but ignores the needs of his soul is similar to Liborio Solis. Even if he wins, he loses

WHERE ARE THE SAMURAI?

When I went to Japan fifty-three years ago, I knew almost nothing about Japan. The only thing I knew was that there were many people who had never heard the gospel. Sometimes I saw airlines commercials on TV. In those commercials, everyone was wearing kimonos and samurai were walking around, so I thought life in Japan was still that kind of life.

When I stepped off the plane at Haneda, I was surprised. Everyone was wearing Western-style clothing and there was not even one samurai. I wondered, "Where are the samurai?" Even now, when I remember that day, I laugh at my ignorance.

Every time I read Hebrews 11:8, I remember that experience. "By faith Abraham, when he was called to go out into a place which he should after receive for an inheritance, obeyed; and <u>he went out, not knowing whither he went</u>."

When God said to Abraham, "Get out of thy country" (Genesis 12:1), "Abraham departed, as the Lord had spoken to him." (Genesis 12:4) This is the image of the person who is fully surrendered to the Lord. There are three words that explain the obedience of Abraham: ANYTHING. ANYWHERE. ANYTIME.

"If it is for the Lord, I will do **anything**. If it is the will of the Lord, I will go **anywhere**. I will follow the leading of the Lord **anytime**." This is the prayer of the Christian who has truly dedicated himself to the Lord.

When Christ said to the first four disciples, "Follow me," they forsook all, and followed him. (Luke 5:11)

WHERE ARE THEY?

When I read the newspaper headline, I was astounded. It said, "MISSING." I had a hard time believing the data in the article. There are 242 people over the age of one hundred who are missing!

My first reaction was, "Where are the families of these people?" As I continued to read the article, I was even more amazed. When asked, "Where is your family member who is over one hundred years old, some of them replied, "We do not know." They do not know! I do not know what you think of their reply, but I could not help but think that their words manifested the depravity of this generation.

The teaching of the Bible concerning elderly people is clear. In the famous Ten Commandments it is written, "Honour thy father and thy mother." Leviticus 19:32 teaches us to "rise up before the hoary head, and honour the face of the old man." In Proverbs 23:22 it is written, "Hearken unto thy father that begat thee, and despise not thy mother when she is old."

If man is nothing more than an animal who was born by chance, the existence of each one of us is an insignificant existence. However, if as the Bible teaches, each one of us is a special creation of God, those of us who have elderly parents must not ignore their existence.

When I consider the lonely life of the 242 people who are missing, my heart is filled with sadness. If it were possible, I would like to find each one of them and tell them, "Even if you are forsaken by your family, there is someone who will never forsake you. That someone is the God who loves you."

WHERE IS MY CAR?

When I went to visit my son and his family who live in Kagoshima, I went to church with them on Sunday. During the pastor's message there was a tremendous sound that shook the church building. After the service I asked my son, "Was that sound an earthquake?" He replied, "No, it was the explosion of the Mount Sakurajima volcano near here."

When we went to the parking lot, I could not find my white car. It was now a black car covered in volcanic ash. All of the cars in the parking lot were covered in black ash.

As I stood there looking at that scene, the words in Romans 5:12 came to my mind. "Wherefore, as by one man sin entered into the world, and death by sin; and so death passed upon all men, for that all have sinned."

When Adam and Eve rebelled against the commandment of God (Genesis chapter three), an explosion like the explosion of Mount Sakurajima occurred in the heart of man. It was an explosion called "sin." Just as all of the cars were covered with black ash as a result of the volcanic explosion, the hearts of all men were blackened by the explosion of sin.

The only thing that can wash away the ash of sin that covers our heart is the blood that Jesus shed when He died on the cross for our sins. "The blood of Jesus Christ his Son cleanseth us from all sin." (First John 1:7)

But there's more. According to Isaiah 61:3, God gives us "beauty for ashes." When we believe in Jesus Christ, God changes our heart covered in the ash of sin into a beautiful heart.

WHERE IS THE GOAL?

Every Sunday I record a TV program called *Shouten* and watch it when I come home from church. (It is similar to the program *Whose Line Is It Anyway?*) On a recent program the comedians were asked, "What marathon would you not like to participate in a second time? I roared with laughter at their answers. One comedian said, "A marathon where they serve only hot tea at the refreshment stand." The answer that amused me the most was, "A marathon where the goal has not been decided yet."

Certainly, the thought of a marathon where no one knows where the goal is makes us laugh, but a life without a goal would be sad. In the marathon called "life," it is important that we follow the example of Paul and run with a specific goal in mind. "I count not myself to have apprehended: but this one thing I do, forgetting those things which are behind, and reaching forth unto those things which are before, I press toward the <u>mark</u> for the prize of the high calling of God in Christ Jesus." (Philippians 3:13-14)

The word "prize" appears in the Bible only two times. The other passage is First Corinthians 9:24-26. "Know ye not that they which run in a race run all, but one receiveth the prize? So run, that ye may obtain. And every man that striveth for the mastery is temperate in all things. Now they do it to obtain a corruptible crown; but we an incorruptible. I therefore so run, <u>not as uncertainly</u>." "Not as uncertainly" – in other words, not knowing where the goal is.

With our eyes on a definite goal, let's run "the race that is set before us." (Hebrews 12:1) Only then will we be able to give the testimony that Paul gave in Second Timothy 4:7. "I have finished my course."

WHEREVER WE GO

In July I preached at the Lighthouse Baptist Church (a church for military personnel serving at the Navy base) in Sasebo. The church provided lodging for me at a hotel in front of the train station. When it was time to go to the evening service, I left the hotel and headed for the parking lot. Suddenly, I heard someone calling, "Pastor Board! Pastor Board!" I looked around and saw Brother Atonakasuji and wife from the Kitakyushu Bible Baptist Church who had come to Sasebo for their vacation. They came out of the train station at the exact time that I came out of the hotel.

In August I took a friend to Nagasaki. We were walking around in Peace Park when I heard someone calling, "Pastor Board! Pastor Board!" I looked around and saw a pastor's family from one of the churches in the Kansai area. They came from Kansai to Peace Park at the exact moment my friend and I were walking there.

Through these two events I learned an important lesson. Wherever I go, someone who knows me may be watching me, so at all times, as the pastor of a church, my conduct should be the proper conduct of a servant of the Lord. This responsibility to conduct ourselves properly wherever we go is also the responsibility of every Christian.

But wait a minute! Even if we go to a place where no one knows us, there is someone watching us. In Jeremiah 23:24 God said, "Can any hide himself in secret places that I shall not see him?" In Psalm 139:7-8 David wrote, "Whither shall I go from thy spirit? or whither shall I flee from thy presence?" If we profess faith in Christ, our way of living should be a way of living that is suitable to our profession.

WHILE I WAS SLEEPING

———— ❧ ————

When I returned from Yahata, there was a notice about a package in my mailbox. (In Japan, the deliveryman will not leave the package on the porch.) That mail was some important documents for which I had been waiting for quite some time, so I immediately called and requested another delivery between 7:00 and 9:00 that night.

In the evening I waited between 7:00 and 9:00, but the documents did not come. I went outside and looked in the mailbox. There was another notice. According to that notice, there had been another attempt to deliver the documents at 7:22. When I saw that, I became angry. I was waiting for the documents all the way from 7:00 to 9:00. Why didn't the deliveryman ring the doorbell?

As I was complaining, I remembered. While I was waiting for the documents, I fell asleep. It was only 5-10 minutes, but right at that time, while I was sleeping, the deliveryman came. Just then, I remembered the words of Christ written in Matthew 24:42. "Watch therefore: for ye know not what hour your Lord doth come."

Many Bible passages teach the second coming of Christ. For example, in John 14:3 Christ said, "If I go and prepare a place for you, I will come again." When will Christ come again? According to Matthew 24:36, only God knows that time. However, when we compare the prophecies about the second coming of Christ with the present condition of the world, we understand that His second coming is near, so let us be vigilant, and let us be diligent in preaching the gospel to as many people as possible. "Therefore let us not sleep, as do others; but let us watch and be sober." (First Thessalonians 5:6)

WHO IS YOUR JESUS?

Matt Murton of the Hanshin Tigers is a zealous Christian. He testifies of Christ every opportunity he has. You can see videos of his testimonies on You Tube.

Recently, during the hero interview after a game, he said, "Jesus is your hope." The reply of the interviewer was quite funny. "The fans think you are Jesus." He had helped the Tigers win several games lately, so he was their savior.

When I heard about this interview from one of the church members, I laughed, but actually I thought the words of the interviewer were sad words. Although there is a true Savior who died on the cross for the sins of all people, most people look for their salvation in another person.

In John 6:66 it is written, "From that time many of his disciples went back, and walked no more with him." In verse 67 Jesus asked His disciples, "Will ye also go away?" This was the wonderful reply of Peter: "Lord, to whom shall we go? thou hast the words of eternal life."

Peter was right. Christ alone has the words of eternal life. Until now, only one person, Jesus Christ, has declared, "He that believeth on me hath everlasting life."

Matt Murton is an excellent baseball player, but he cannot be our "savior". The Bible clearly states, "Neither is there salvation in any other: for there is none other name under heaven given among men, whereby we must be saved." (Acts 4:12) If you are searching for the forgiveness of sin and eternal life, come to Christ, the only true Savior.

WHO TAUGHT THE FIRST CRANE?

———— ❧ ————

When I went to Nagashima in December, Pastor Kishimoto took me to Izumi to see the cranes. Every year, in October, over 10,000 cranes migrate from Siberia to the town of Izumi.

There are other birds who migrate like these cranes. Every year, many swallows migrate from Argentina to the town of Capistrano in California. They arrive on the same day, March 19 and leave on the same day, October 23, every year.

Some scientists say that the cranes learn migration from their parents, but this opinion raises a big question. Who taught the first crane? The Bible teaches that the migration of the cranes is not something that they learned but rather an instinct that God gave to the cranes when He created them. In Genesis 1:21 it is written, "God created great whales, and every living creature that moveth, which the waters brought forth abundantly, after their kind, and <u>every winged fowl</u> after his kind: and God saw that it was good." When God created the first cranes, in order to protect them, He gave them the instinct to migrate in the winter.

The dictionary defines instinct as "natural-born knowledge." Even if we do agree that the second crane learned migration from his father, how will we explain the natural knowledge of the first crane?

The word "crane" appears twice in the Bible, in Isaiah 38:14 and Jeremiah 8:7. The Jeremiah passage reads like this: " Yea, the stork in the heaven knoweth her appointed times; and the turtle and <u>the crane</u> and the swallow observe the time of their coming; but my people know not the judgment of the Lord."

WINE, GOLF, AND HOT SPRINGS

When friends come from America to visit me, I always explain, "There are three ways for men to have fellowship in Japan. First, we could go to the bar and drink wine, but I do not drink wine, so that is out. Second, we could play golf, but I have never played golf, and even if I wanted to, in Japan golf is too expensive for the salary of a missionary, so golf too is out of the question. There is only one thing left to do. We can go bathe in a hot spring. Grab your towel and come with me."

In America, men do not normally bathe together naked, so when my friends hear this, they are somewhat hesitant, but they go with me. Later, they usually say something like this, "At first, I was embarrassed, but I am glad I went. I feel great!"

We all recognize the necessity for fellowship with friends; however, if fellowship with friends is necessary, how much more necessary is it for Christians to fellowship with one another. In Acts 2:42 we can see four characteristics of a healthy church. "They continued stedfastly in the apostles' doctrine and <u>fellowship</u>, and in breaking of bread, and in prayers."

Some people would limit this fellowship to reading the Bible, praying, and discussing church-related matters together. However, our fellowship could consist also of participating in delightful activities such as meals and games together. We should take advantage of various methods to spend time together and encourage one another.

"Behold, how good and how pleasant it is for brethren to dwell together in unity!" (Psalm 133:1)

YOU

I prepared fifty decision cards for Summer Camp. After I had printed them all, I noticed a terrible mistake. Instead of using the word *anata* (you), I had used the word *anta*. In this area, there are people who use *anta*, but it is a very colloquial word. The courteous word is *anata*, so I threw away the cards and printed new ones.

When we speak to another person in English, the only word is YOU. However, in Japanese, there are various words – *anata, kimi, omae, kisama, anatagata* (plural) and *anta*. There may be more, but I know only these six.

The word *anata* (you) appears in the Japanese Bible 8410 times. Different than the gods of other religions, the God of the Bible desires a personal relationship with each one of us. God made many wonderful promises to the person who believes in Jesus Christ.

"I am with YOU always." (Matthew 28:20)

"I go to prepare a place for YOU." (John 14:2)

"Peace I leave with YOU, my peace I give unto YOU." (John 14:27)

"Come unto me, all ye that labour and are heavy laden, and I will give YOU rest." (Matthew 11:28)

God loves YOU. Christ died on the cross for YOU. Please receive the salvation and promises that God has prepared for YOU. Please experience the personal relationship that God wants to have with YOU.

"YOU CAN EAT ANYTHING
YOU WANT, BUT . . ."

I went to the hospital to visit Brother Yamaguchi. Just as I arrived there, a nurse was conducting a class on nutrition, so I listened to it with Brother and Sister Yamaguchi. The main portion of her talk stressed the importance of decreasing salt intake, but the words that remained in my mind were, "You can eat anything you want, BUT . . ." Her words ended with "but"; however, I knew the rest of the sentence. "You can eat anything you want, but if you want to protect your health, you will be careful what you eat."

In chapter eight of First Corinthians, Paul wrote similar words to the believers in Corinth. They were arguing over the matter of eating meat offered to idols, specifically, whether or not it was okay for a Christian to eat that meat. In verse four he wrote, "As concerning therefore the eating of those things that are offered in sacrifice unto idols, we know that an idol is nothing in the world, and that there is none other God but one." In other words, "Idols are not gods, so it is okay to eat meat offered to them."

However, just as there was a BUT in the explanation of the nurse, there was a BUT in the explanation of Paul. "Howbeit there is not in every man that knowledge: for some with conscience of the idol unto this hour eat it as a thing offered unto an idol; and their conscience being weak is defiled." (verse 7)

The conclusion of Paul is written in verse nine. "**But** take heed lest by any means this liberty of yours become a stumblingblock to them that are weak." Christ has given wonderful freedom to us, but let us be careful lest that freedom becomes a stumbling block to another Christian.

"YOU DID OKAY"

(Cristy gave me permission to write this message,) I took Cristy Wyatt to the driver's license bureau four times. She failed all four times. When she failed the first time, she cried. She did not cry the second, third, and fourth times, but she went home frustrated.

When the fifth test was over, she was told to get out of the car. She thought she had failed again. But the examiner said, "You did OK." In that instant, she forgot all about the tears and frustration. Her face was overflowing with joy.

When I saw this, I remembered the parable of Christ in chapter 25 of Matthew. A master gave money to three of his servants and went on a trip. Two of them were able to increase his money, so he said to them, "Well done, thou good and faithful servant."

In the same way, Christians desire to use the talent that God has given them to bring glory to His name and live a life that is pleasing to Him. However, there are times when we do not succeed. There are times when we are frustrated. There are times when we cry.

However, if we faithfully serve the Lord with all our strength, we too will hear the words that bring the greatest joy to Christians. "Well done, thou good and faithful servant. You did OK." When we hear those words, we shall forget all about the trials, the failures, and the tears and sense the most wonderful joy. "Blessed are ye, when men shall revile you, and persecute you, and shall say all manner of evil against you falsely, for my sake. Rejoice and be exceeding glad: for great is your reward in heaven." (Matthew 5:11-12)

"YOU WON'T GO TO HEAVEN TODAY"

I have several problems with my health, so every month I have to go to my primary care doctor and my urologist for exams. I have been going to my primary care doctor for many years, so we like to joke with one another.

When I went to see him recently, after checking my blood pressure, he said, "You won't go to heaven today." Because he has been taking care of my health for so long, I replied, "I want to go to heaven the same day you go." The doctor and nurses all laughed.

Later, I began thinking about his words. "You won't go to heaven today." Actually, even though my health is not so serious that I might die today, the time of my death will not be decided by me or my doctor.

According to the Bible, God holds our breath in His hand. (Daniel 5:23) Acts 17:28 states this truth in even clearer words. "For in him we live, and move, and have our being."

I praise the doctors who try to help us live long lives. I am thankful to them. If not for their ability and knowledge, I probably would have died five years ago. The God who holds our breath in His hand used them to prolong my life.

Even if the doctor says, "You won't go to heaven today," there is no doctor who knows when we shall depart this world. The only one who knows that is the God who gave us life to begin with and holds our breath in His hands. Knowing this, ought we not to live in such a way that it would be okay even if we did go to heaven today?

YUBI KIRI GENMAN

The first time I saw children hook their little fingers and say "*yubi kiri genman*," and make a promise to one another, I thought it was a very cute custom. I have continued to think so for forty-three years.

However, recently a friend taught me the rest of that pledge and its meaning. The rest of the pledge is *uso tsuitara, hari sen bon nomasu, yubi kitta*. "If I break my promise, I will swallow a thousand needles and cut off my finger." I was shocked. I no longer think *yubi kiri genman* is a cute custom. I think it is terrifying.

Of course, I understand that the person who breaks a promise does not actually have to swallow a thousand needles and cut off his finger. I think the *yubi kiri genman* custom is a cute way of teaching the importance of keeping promises.

The Bible teaches that the words of Christians should be "sound" words. "In all things shewing thyself a pattern of good works: in doctrine shewing uncorruptness, gravity, sincerity, <u>Sound speech, that cannot be condemned</u>; that he that is of the contrary part may be ashamed, having no evil thing to say of you." The words of a Christian who breaks a promise brings shame not only to the individual himself but also to his church.

Of course, if keeping a promise you made to another person is important, how much more important is it for us to keep our promises to God. "When thou shalt vow a vow unto the LORD thy God, thou shalt not slack to pay it: for the LORD thy God will surely require it of thee; and it would be sin in thee." (Deuteronomy 23:21)

221 AND S21

When I went to the JBBF Summer Camp in August, I took a ferryboat from Moji. It was the second time I spent the night on a ferryboat. Several years ago, my family took a ferryboat from Fukuoka to Okinawa. We slept in a large room with many other people. This time, I reserved my own room, so as soon as I boarded the ferry, I began searching for room 221.

It took a while, but I finally found my room and opened the door, but there was another person in the room. At first, I intended to show him my ticket and ask him to leave the room, but I decided to find one of the stewards and have him do it for me. While I was searching for a steward, I looked at my ticket again. It was not room 221. It was room S21. My weak eyes saw a [2] instead of an [S].

If I had tried to make the person in room 221 get out of the room, a terrible incident might have occurred. Likewise, if there were even one instance in the Bible, the foundation of our faith, where even one letter was incorrect, the result would be terrible. That is why the words of Christ in Matthew 5:18 give us assurance. "For verily I say unto you, Till heaven and earth pass, one jot or one tittle shall in no wise pass from the law, till all be fulfilled."

Furthermore, in Luke 16:17 Christ said, "It is easier for heaven and earth to pass, than one tittle of the law to fail." If God is protecting even the jots and tittles of His Word, Christians can walk with confidence the path that the Word lights up for us. (Psalm 119:105) "Being born again, not of corruptible seed, but of incorruptible, by the word of God, which liveth and abideth for ever." (First Peter 1:23)

30,651

For fourteen years in a row, I have read the same newspaper article that saddens me greatly. It is the annual report of the number of suicides in Japan the previous year. Last year, 30,651 Japanese committed suicide. The number inside this number that especially saddens is the number of students who committed suicide – 1029. It was the first time that the number of student suicides exceeded one thousand.

There are three main reasons why over 30,000 people choose dying over living – health problems, financial problems, and family problems.

The stories of four people who committed suicide are written in the Bible. Saul (First Samuel 31:4) Ahithofel (Second Samuel 17:23) Zimri (First Kings 16:18) Of course, the most well-known suicide is the suicide of Judas (Matthew 27:3-5)

You have probably seen the Kanebo cosmetics commercial – For Beautiful Human Life. Of course, everyone desires a "beautiful life," but when problems pile up one upon another, there are times when life is not very beautiful.

If you have ever considered suicide even once, please remember two things. First, life is a precious gift from God. (Acts 17:25) According to Psalm 139:13-16, each one of us was created and fashioned by God.

Second, even though we may think that suicide is the best solution of our problems, there is a better solution. Trust in the God who made this promise in Psalm 50:15. "Call upon me in the day of trouble: I will deliver thee."